INTERESTING STORIES FOR CURIOUS KIDS

A Fascinating Collection of the Most Interesting, Unbelievable, and Craziest Stories on Earth!

BILL O'NEILL

ISBN: 978-1-64845-081-5

DON'T FORGET YOUR FREE BOOKS

Contents

Introduction

Welcome to *Interesting Stories for Curious Kids: A Fascinating Collection of the Most Interesting, Unbelievable, and Craziest Stories on Earth!* This book will introduce you to some of the strangest facts on our incredible planet but in a way that is fun for you! You'll definitely learn an enormous amount reading this book, but I guarantee you'll never be bored.

Since you have a busy life with family, friends, school, and hobbies, the way you read this book is entirely up to you. You can read it from cover to cover like a traditional book, or you can skip around and not miss a thing. Each of the stories is also fairly short, so you don't have to spend a lot of time reading them.

The stories in this book come from different categories of human life, but the important thing is they are written to appeal to kids your age. That's right; this book was written with the interests of kids your age in mind! Some of the research was even done by kids your age! So when you read about these historical stories, it will also be something you'll find fun. For instance, you'll read about some of the most powerful kids in history, from ancient Egyptian pharaohs to Chinese and Japanese emperors. You'll also learn about how the Vikings invented sledding, skiing, and skating. And what about school? Well, you'll learn how schools a long time ago were different, and sometimes the same, as they are today.

Plus, for all you science fans, don't worry, we've got you covered! There are plenty of fun science stories in here that answer some questions you and your friends have no doubt discussed. What's the smartest animal in the world? How many bones are in the human body? How are llamas related to camels? How do parrots talk? Even if science isn't your best subject, you're sure to find something you like and information that you didn't know.

There are also a few fun science experiments that you can do to impress your friends and family. We show you how it's impossible to crush an egg in the palm of your hand and how to mummify a hotdog—yes; you read that last part correctly!

Dive in and read about some of your favorite movies, books, and entertainers to learn how they got their starts. You may be surprised that some of your favorite movies were remakes of movies that your parents—and even your grandparents—once thought were cool.

Finally, kids all over the world like a good scary story from time to time, so we have a few here you are certain to like, plus a few stories that defy categorization.

So sit back, relax, and open the pages of this book to travel into another world where learning is fun. Once you read a few of the stories in this book, you're sure to impress your friends and maybe even win a few arguments.

But more than anything - just remember to have fun!

The Hero Cat

Dogs and cats may be the most popular pets, but few would doubt that dogs usually get top billing. After all, you've heard the saying, "a dog is man's best friend," right? The reason for that probably has to do with a cat's personality more than anything. Those of you who have cats know what I mean.

Cats like to eat.

Cats like to sleep.

Generally speaking, cats like to do whatever they want and don't really like their humans telling them what to do. Notice I said, "their humans"? Well, that's because you never really own a cat. They may choose to like you, or let you pet them, but they're always totally independent creatures.

But there are always exceptions to every rule.

For instance, take the example of the hero cat Tara. A feisty tabby cat, Tara was unfortunately left on the streets of Bakersfield, California in 2008. Things are tough for cats living on the streets, even cats as tough as Tara. So when Roger and Erica Triantafilo noticed that a cute kitty was following them on their walk, they became a little concerned.

"Whose cat is this?" they wondered.

Roger and Erica brought the cat to their house, gave her some food, and cleaned her up. It was obvious that the cat had been on the streets for some time. However, she was very sweet, so the Triantafilos thought 'well goodness, she must belong to someone'.

They asked their neighbors and even put out some flyers stating that they had found a presumably lost tabby cat. No one came forward. It was 2008 and the economy was bad, so it's anyone's guess as to how the cat ended up on the streets.

But it soon became clear that the cat had found a new home with the Triantafilos. The couple's 4-year-old son, Jeremy, grew especially close to the cat. The family finally decided to adopt the lovable cat and name her "Tara."

Tara followed Jeremy around like a puppy and she quickly began helping the boy come out of his shell. You see, Jeremy has autism so he often had a difficult time expressing himself or making friends.

Then, on May 13, 2014, the incident happened that made Tara the world-famous "Hero Cat."

It began as just another day in the Triantafilo's house. Jeremy was playing in the driveway of the family home, with Tara basking in the sun nearby, alternating between watching birds and Jeremy.

Suddenly, out of nowhere, a big vicious dog came running into the Triantafilo's driveway and attacked Jeremy in an unprovoked full-on attack. Jeremy was confused, scared, and in pain as the Chow mix tore into his leg. His mother came running to protect him, but before she got there, Tara sprang into action!

The frisky feline flung her body onto the aggressive doggo and then chased him around the family's car and out of the driveway. Erica picked Jeremy up and the three then retreated to their house to catch their breaths and wits. After bringing Jeremy to the emergency room to get ten stitches, the Triantafilos uploaded the security camera footage of the attack to YouTube, where it immediately went viral by getting almost 17 million views in 48 hours.

Tara became an international celebrity overnight. She threw out the first pitch to a minor league baseball game (sort of), dropped the puck for a minor league hockey game (sort of), and made numerous media appearances with her family.

About a year later, Tara was probably one of the best known and most traveled cats of all time, having visited countries in Europe, Asia, and Latin America. And few will deny that Tara deserved all the attention. After all, she potentially saved Jeremy's life, proving that a cat *can* be a person's best friend… and a hero.

Growing Pains

As you grow up through your 'tween years and become a teen, you've no doubt heard the term "growing pains" at least once in life. "Growing pains" is actually a "double entendre" (I know that term sounds like a big deal, but it just means "double meaning"). One meaning of the term is more metaphorical and relates to the pressures and stresses of growing up. For instance, losing your first boyfriend or girlfriend can be a growing pain, as can getting braces, having to switch schools, not making a team, or even getting a bad grade.

They are all the negative aspects of growing up, so they are called "growing pains."

But the term growing pains actually has an older, more practical definition. Some of you reading this may have experienced some true growing pains. If you have, don't be worried because they're perfectly natural!

Growing pains refer to pains and aches that kids up to the age of 12 experience primarily in their legs and sometimes their arms. The pains usually take place at night and can get so bad that they can wake a kid up, but they usually go away quickly in the morning.

If you've experienced growing pains, you're not alone. Up to 40% of all kids have growing pains, so if you feel them, don't get worried. But, be concerned if you feel them repeatedly. As the name says, they tend to go away when you hit your teens and stop growing.

But you may be interested to know that—other than the fact that they stop around the time you quit growing—growing pains have little else to do with growth.

Growing pains were first written about in 1823 by a French doctor named Marcel Duchamp, although he didn't know much about them, other than that they were only seen in children. He also didn't know the causes. Many doctors and scientists thought that growing pains were the result of children having rheumatic fever. But as medical science grew in the 1900s, so too did knowledge about growing pains.

Scientists eventually learned that growing pains weren't caused by rheumatic fever, or any other type of illness. When they noticed that most teenagers quit having them, they began to think that the condition was caused by the human body naturally growing.

But more recent research has revealed that isn't the truth either.

Scientists still don't truly know the causes of growing pains. Some think that they happen when kids play too hard, and others believe they come from poor posture. Some scientists have argued that growing pains may be a symptom of other conditions. For the vast majority of kids who experience growing pains, though, they are quite harmless.

So if you wake up with your legs aching a little, remember that those pains should be gone by the time you're in your teens. Now as far as those growing pains dealing with girlfriends and boyfriends, grades, and parents—well, those may last a little longer!

Poor Alexei and Anastasia

Things were tough in Russia in 1917. The country was in the middle of World War I against Germany and Austria-Hungary. War in itself, is often bad enough, but the Russians were doing very poorly on the battlefield. It wasn't that the Germans and Austrians were necessarily better soldiers, but more that the Russians had a tough time supplying their troops. The trains that brought supplies to the front were old and unreliable, and often there simply wasn't enough food to begin with, or guns and ammunition.

It's kind of hard to win a war without ammunition, right?

Well, as you can imagine, things in Russia itself weren't much better. The people were poor, unemployment was high, and there were constant social tensions between the different classes and ethnic groups (not everyone in Russia was Russian). All of these problems were being stirred up by the communists, who wanted to overthrow the Tsar (the Russian word for emperor—think "Caesar").

The communists said, "See how well the Tsar and his family live while the people suffer!"

They did have a point. Tsar Nicholas II and his family were living pretty well, at least until March 15, 1917.

Nicholas II was the last Tsar of the Romanov Dynasty, which began ruling Russia in 1613. This was quite an accomplishment when you consider that Russia had some major problems during that particular 300-year period. There were civil wars, attempted revolutions, and one Tsar was even assassinated! So by the time World War I started in 1914, it was clear to many that Russia was headed for even more problems.

But Nicholas, his wife Alexandra, together with their four daughters and one son didn't seem to notice.

You see, the Romanovs spent most of their time in the royal palace and knew very little about what was taking place around them in Russia. In fact, the Romanovs probably knew more about the other royal families in Europe than they did about people in their own country. You see, it may seem strange, but the Romanovs were related to most of the other royal families in Europe at the time. Yes, even those they were at war with!

Both Nicholas and Alexandra were just as much from German royal families as they were from the Russian nobility. Nicholas was also part of the Danish royalty. The couple was even related to the English royal family.

Needless to say, the Romanovs were a bit out of touch with the Russian people, but that didn't mean that they were without problems of their own. Alexei, who was the crown prince (the next in line to be the Tsar), suffered from the rare disease hemophilia. Hemophilia is a disease where the blood doesn't clot properly, which means a simple cut can turn into a life-threatening wound because it won't stop bleeding.

Due to his rare condition, Alexei was placed into even more of a bubble, constantly watched, with nurses and doctors attending to him - 24 hours a day, seven days a week. But his family was there too and by all accounts, they were quite close. The pictures and even film from the era show a loving family. Alexei's sisters, especially the youngest, Anastasia, played with and watched out for him.

But all of that came crashing down quickly when Tsar Nicholas decided to enter World War I against Germany and the Central Powers. Russia just wasn't prepared for a long war and as the battlefield losses began to pile up, so too did the protests.

Nicholas abdicated from the throne on March 15, 1917, and soon after he and his family were placed under house arrest. Even after having everything taken from them, the Romanovs tried to make the best of their situation. Pictures of the Romanovs show that they remained close and in relatively good spirits until July 17, 1918.

On that fateful day, the communist wardens of the Romanovs herded them into a basement of a house in Yekaterinburg, Russia and executed them. It was said that the girls and their mother were trying to make the sign of the cross as they were shot to death. Anastasia and Maria lived through the initial barrage of gunfire because they had the family jewels sewed in their corsets which deflected some of the bullets. But the executioners finished them off with bayonets.

That sad scene marked the end of Romanov rule in Russia and the beginning of communist rule, which would last more than 70 years. The Romanovs are today remembered as a loving family and true believers in the Christian faith. Because of that, the Russian Orthodox Church made Nicholas, Alexandra, and all their children saints in the year 2000.

Make Your Own Invisible Ink

Spies have been around for probably as long as there have been humans. I'd guess that even in the Pre-historic Era when people were living in caves, cavemen did some spying on their rivals to see who had the best tools and weapons.

And as human societies developed and became more advanced, so too did the spy game.

Spying eventually became a legitimate—or somewhat legitimate—profession, in which the specialized tools and tactics that were created were known as *tradecraft*. Tradecraft includes everything from the gadgets you see in James Bond movies to simple things that you and your friends can do…like invisible ink.

Yes, that's right, invisible ink!

I'm sure you've heard about invisible ink in a movie or read about it in a book, but it's not just fiction. Spies really did use invisible ink to send secret messages! It was a popular method because it was so easy to do. The spy simply took a liquid that produced the ink, wrote it on a paper, and then wrote a regular, innocent message on the paper with pencil or ink.

Easy enough, right? Well, let's try it.

First, you'll need a piece of paper, of course. Next, you need to have access to an iron, oven, or radiator. Don't worry; you won't be turning the heat up very high. You'll also need a toothpick or Q-tip. Finally, the most important ingredient is the actual ink. You can find most of these ingredients in your family's home.

Fruit juices with a high acidic level work great, so that includes apple juice, orange juice, and perhaps best is lemon juice. Onion juice can also work well if you don't mind shedding a few tears! Vinegar is also another popular form of invisible ink.

Urine has also been used by spies as a form of invisible ink. Yeah, I know it's gross and I wouldn't recommend it, but I had to mention it!

Pour some of whatever liquid you are using for invisible ink into a small cup, dip your toothpick or Q-tip into the cup, and start writing your message on the piece of paper. You then let it dry and the words simply disappear.

When you are ready to see your secret message again, with the iron on the lowest setting, run it over the paper. Or you can lay the paper on a radiator or in an oven set below 300 °F.

Watch as you see the words you wrote quickly reveal themselves! Don't get upset if your first secret message doesn't look very clean. It takes a little practice to write with invisible ink and you may want to experiment with different types of ink. With a little practice, though, in no time you'll be impressing your friends and family with secret messages that would make any spy proud.

Bazooka Joe Gets a Facelift

A long time ago, back when your parents—and more like your grandparents—were your age, Bazooka Joe was *the* coolest candy for kids. You see, back before the internet existed, and even before every home had a television, Bazooka Joe gum combined candy with a comic strip. It proved to be an ingenious marketing ploy, making it one of the most popular candies in the world for decades.

As some of you probably know, Bazooka Joe is still around, although it's definitely been through some changes.

The kids of America were first introduced to Bazooka Joe gum in the 1950s. As they peeled back the paper of each individually-wrapped square piece of gum, they were delighted to find the comic strip *Bazooka Joe and His Gang*. Each strip included a short, approximately four-frame comic story in which Joe and his friends would observe a situation and tell a joke.

And if you collected enough *Bazooka Joe and His Gang* comic strips, you could mail them to an address for a prize. The prize was usually something cheap, like a pair of sunglasses, a plastic ring, or a plastic telescope. But hey, it was a good marketing ploy because it kept kids buying more and more of the gum.

Bazooka Joe quickly became one of the most popular kids' candies in America and spread to just about every country in the world during the 1960s.

But as the times changed, Bazooka Joe had a difficult time keeping up with the competition.

The introduction of sugary, soft bubble gums aimed at kids, such as Bubble Yum, Bubblicious, and Hubba Bubba, in the late 1970s, cut into Bazooka Joe's profits. Still, Bazooka Joe was able to hold on because kids could buy single pieces at five or ten cents apiece.

Bazooka Joe himself even had a makeover in the 1990s to keep up with the look of that time, but by the 2000s, he just wasn't very popular anymore. Kids that were your age and older found the humor kind of corny. And who wants to save up a bunch of comic strips to mail somewhere for a cheap prize, right?

Your generation is certainly much more tech-savvy than previous generations. The owners of Bazooka Joe realized this and discontinued the outdated comic strip and prizes in 2012.

Those of you who enjoy a good piece of gum from time to time will know that Bazooka Joe is still around. And you'll also know that, instead of corny comic strips, the packaging on each piece has puzzles and codes for video games you can unlock on the Bazooka Joe website. Bazooka Joe and his friends can still be seen occasionally on the packaging, but the emphasis is on things that are more modern that you like.

You see, even though you may be years away from voting, the purchasing power of your generation is strong enough to change the way a company presents its product. And as much as Bazooka Joe has changed, he'll probably go through many more changes by the time your kids start chewing it.

Road Trip Games

Some of you reading this have been on long road trips with your family during summer vacation, or maybe it was on a long drive to a family member's home during the holidays. I probably don't have to tell you that some of these trips can be quite boring and annoying.

Maybe your dad or mom didn't want to stop when you did.

Or maybe your little brother or sister slept and snored most of the time—or worse - wouldn't shut up. Or even worse, couldn't quit passing gas!

Don't worry, though. You have just been through, and will probably go through again, what many kids have experienced for decades. The long and often boring or annoying road trip is something that American kids have experienced since the 1950s, so your parents and grandparents know the feeling.

But it doesn't always have to be annoying or boring.

There are plenty of fun word games that you, your siblings, and your parents can play to pass the time while you whiz down the highway. I'll go through a few of the more popular games and a few that I like playing. So no doubt, as you read this, you'll probably think of a few new ones yourself.

Perhaps the most popular road trip game is the "License Plate Game." There are different variations of this game, as is the case with most road trip games. Most usually involve the

15

players identifying and shouting out the location of license plates they see. Someone keeps score, with the points for plates usually varying according to distance.

So let's say you're driving through Minnesota. All cars with Minnesota license plates only get one point, but surrounding states—Iowa, Wisconsin, North Dakota, and South Dakota—might get two points. States outside those might get three points and those from the coasts—New York, California, and Texas for example—could get four points. Canadian plates can get five points.

The big point totals, though, are reserved for Alaska, Hawaii, and Puerto Rico. If you see a car with one of those plates, you usually get six points or more.

The License Plate Game is not only a fun way to pass the time, but it's also educational so I'm sure your parents will like it!

Another fun game that my 12-year-old niece once taught me on a road trip is called "Alphabet People," although you can come up with your own name for it.

Alphabet People works like this: the first person in the car starts with the letter "A", and has to think of a name, occupation, and place that all start with "A." So, you could say: "My name is Allen, I'm an author, and I live in Allentown, Pennsylvania." Then the next person could say: "My name is Bonnie, I'm a botanist, and I live in Brooklyn, New York."

And you keep going until you reach your destination or decide to play another game.

Another game, one that I like to do with my friends and family, I call "Either Or."

Either Or involves a person stating two things that are similar, yet different. Each person then has to choose one until it ends up with the person who started with the two terms. So if I started the game, I could say something like, "*Star Wars* or *Star Trek*." Once everyone states their preference, the next person states two new terms, perhaps "Cake or Pie," or "Hamburgers or Hotdogs," or "Pickups or Cars." There are nearly endless possibilities. Just remember that the terms have to be similar but at the same time different enough that people will rarely hesitate with their choices.

Either Or is a good way to learn something new about your friends and family.

These are just three games you can play while you're on a long road trip. I'm sure that when you think about it, you can come up with even more.

How Many Lassies Were There?

Few would argue that the most famous dog to star in movies and TV was Lassie, the lovable, loyal, and tenacious collie. Lassie first made her—or his (we'll get to that in a moment)—big-screen debut in the 1943 film *Lassie Come Home* and then went on to star in dozens of films and TV shows well into the 1970s. After the 1970s, Lassie's popularity faded a bit, but she's been brought back from time to time in different shows.

It's not the same dog from 1943, of course. So how many dogs have played Lassie?

Before we get to that answer, let's take a look at the first dog to play Lassie, which was 'Pal'. If you're thinking, "Pal sure sounds like a boy dog's name" then you're on to something because Pal was a male collie. All of the dogs after Pal to play Lassie were also males. The reason why males always played Lassie (which, of course, is very much a girl's name) was because male collies have a very distinct color and pattern on their coats.

After auditioning hundreds of dogs, Pal was determined to be the smartest, the easiest for people to get along with, and the best looking. Pal faithfully filled the role of Lassie on-screen until he passed away in 1958 at the age of 18. In dog years Pal/Lassie was 85.

In all those years Lassie was living it up in Hollywood, he had the time and money to start a family. And when Lassie finally died, the torch of Lassie was passed to his son, Pal Junior. Junior carried on the tradition faithfully and in fact, all of the collies who played Lassie in the six original movies and the television series were descended from Pal. There were also stunt dogs and stand-ins that played Lassie, while other collies not related to Pal played Lassie in later movies.

The exact number of dogs that have played Lassie isn't known for sure, but it's believed there were about a dozen. And all of them were boys!

Child Soldiers

Making your way through your 'tweens into your teen years can be a tough thing. You're under a lot of pressure to make friends, do well in school, and behave well at home. Your schoolwork is getting harder and harder and it's often difficult keeping up with the latest fashions, fads, and music. But if you keep your head up and remain positive, you'll find that due to a couple of reasons, things aren't so bad after all.

First, you'll be through these awkward years quicker than you think. And trust me, once you are through these years, you'll look back at it all and laugh. You'll laugh about the clothing styles and music that you once thought were cool and you'll laugh about the fact that anyone at your school thought that one boy or girl was the coolest thing since ice cream.

Second, you can be glad you're not a child soldier.

War has been around as long as there have been people, and unfortunately, children have been caught directly in the middle of wars, time and time again. Usually, children have been the victims of war, being kidnapped by conquering armies, or killed in the crossfire, but sometimes they have taken part in the fighting. Usually, it has been the boys who have done the fighting, but girls have also picked up swords, bows, and guns throughout history.

Although international agreements and laws forbid armies from using children in warfare, there are thousands of children right now fighting throughout the world. Most of these child soldiers are in the continent of Africa, where war and conflict are common. It is estimated that more than 17,000 children have been recruited to fight in the country of South Sudan in Africa alone.

You're probably wondering, "How does a kid become a solider?" Well, that's a good question with many different answers.

You may find this hard to believe, but many children have actually willingly joined armies. It's important to remember that these kids have grown up in a very different world to yours. Many of them were brought up and lived in a level of poverty that most people today wouldn't understand and in places where war is common.

Many of these kids have lost one or both of their parents to war, so joining an army gives them a new family. In turn, the army provides them with food and shelter.

But some of these kids had no choice.

The governments of Somalia, Sudan, and South Sudan often conscript (draft or force) children into their armies. There are also several rebel groups and private armies that capture children and force them to fight in this region. During the 1990s, a rebel army in the nation of Sierra Leone called the Revolutionary United Front (RUF) became notorious for taking children from their parents, some as young as five, and forcing them to fight.

Thankfully, the RUF was defeated in 2002 and most of the children were freed. But what would be their future after this horrible period of their life?

International laws and agreements have greatly reduced the number of child soldiers throughout the world, but it's estimated that more than 30,000 still remain armed and ready to fight in Africa alone.

So the next time your parents get on you about doing your homework, or some kid makes fun of you because you don't have the newest, coolest shoes, just remember that there are thousands of child soldiers around the world who'd love to be in your shoes.

The Beautiful Hitchhiker

Before we get into our next story, it's important to define what a "scary story" is and what's an "urban legend" or an "urban myth." A scary story is simply as the name states, any story that can scare those who hear it. These stories can involve ghosts, aliens, monsters, crazed killers, psychic powers, or just about anything that can scare the average person.

An urban myth, or an urban legend (whichever name you prefer) is a story that has been told so many times that people believe it, but there's really no way of proving if it ever happened. The reality is that both scary stories and urban myths can be true, although they usually aren't. More likely, they are based on some truth and then grossly over-exaggerated.

Our next story is one part scary story and one part urban myth. It'll be up to you to decide if any, or all of it is true. But be warned, it's more than a little creepy!

On a cold spring night in a rural area of the Midwest, a man named John was driving home from his job on the nightshift at a factory. It had just started to rain when John noticed a young woman with long dark hair, wearing a white dress, walking alongside the road.

Not wanting to see the woman get wet, he pulled over and asked her if she needed a ride. The woman just stared at John for a few seconds with a lost sort of look but then got in the passenger seat. She put her purse down and began looking ahead, as if seeing something in the distance that she dreaded.

She told John that she was going to a farmhouse about three miles down the road.

John tried to make small talk with the woman, but she only stared ahead.

Soon he arrived at the mysterious woman's house, but before he could say anything, she had already gone inside. "Oh well," John thought, "I guess she was cold and wet and just wanted to go inside."

John went home, had something to eat, watched TV, went to bed, and forgot all about the mysterious woman until he was driving home from work the next night.

"I wondered to myself, who that beautiful woman was?" John thought to himself.

He then noticed the beautiful woman's purse. John pulled over to the side of the road to see if she had an ID. He wasn't trying to be nosy; he just that he wanted to return the woman's purse.

"Lydia Penn. 1200 Osiris Road," it read.

John then remembered that the address was the exact location where he had dropped the mysterious woman off the night before, so he drove there.

But what happened next was truly terrifying and mystifying!

John knocked on the door and after a few seconds, an old woman answered.

"This purse belongs to Lydia Penn, I believe she lives here," said John to the woman.

"You're the fourth one," the woman said as she took the purse from John's hands.

Confused about what was happening, John asked what she meant.

"It was 20 years ago this night, on a night like this, that my beautiful Lydia died in a car accident about three miles down the road." The woman continued, "Ever since that time, every five years she reappears to a young man like you."

The old woman went to the kitchen, poured a drink of whiskey, and looked at John.

"You don't believe me, do you?"

John was dumbfounded, confused, and unable to answer.

The old woman took a drink and said, "Go to the cemetery across the road and see her in the third row." The woman then handed John a red rose. "Give this to her. She always loved roses."

Still shocked by the story he had just heard, John left the home with the rose in his hand. He looked at his car and seriously considered leaving this entire crazy situation, but then he looked across the road at the cemetery and was compelled to enter it.

John went to the third row and sure enough, there it was on a gravestone: LYDIA PENN.

Frozen by a combination of fear and confusion, John wanted to run, but then he noticed he was still clutching the rose. John placed the rose on Lydia's grave and went home. He continued to use that same road to go to and from work for several years, but never again saw the beautiful, mysterious woman.

Some people will say this is nothing but a ghost story, and others will say it's an urban myth that was based on something real. Just remember, if you're ever driving alone through the rural Midwest and see a beautiful woman with long dark hair wearing a white dress walking alongside the road, it may be a ghostly apparition from another world.

But don't worry. She only wants a ride home, a rose, and a visit to her grave.

Morris the Cat Had More Than Nine Lives

If you ask your parents what was the most famous animal when they were your age, you may be surprised to learn it was a cat. Yes, he was an orange tabby cat who was the spokes cat for the '9Lives' brand of cat food.

Said to be the "world's most finicky cat," if Morris liked 9Lives then your cat was sure to like it. The original 9Lives commercials with Morris the Cat began airing in 1968, but there's a whole lot more to how Morris became a movie star and how he was able to live so long.

Morris's early life was tough. He was abandoned and found himself in a Chicago animal shelter, facing almost certain death, when animal handler Bob Martwick "discovered" him. Martwick had been hired by an advertising company to find a cat that would be the face of the 9Lives brand of cat food. The cat had to be nice looking, yet very average and not unlike most American cats.

The most important, and perhaps most difficult, requirement was that the cat had to be trainable.

I'm sure many of you reading this have cats at home, in which case you know how difficult it is to train a cat to do anything. It's not that cats are dumb, in fact quite the opposite is true. Cats simply do things when and how they want to do them.

But maybe because Morris had lived such a rough life and he knew that he was facing a nice, comfortable existence with all the 9Lives he could eat, he proved to be a fairly trainable cat.

Morris lived with Martwick as his pet and was the face of 9Lives until he died in 1978.

If you're a parent reading this, you may be thinking to yourself, "I remember seeing Morris the Cat in commercials during the 1980s."

Well, your mind isn't playing tricks on you. Just like with Lassie, Martwick went and got another Morris the Cat, who also lived with him and played the cat until the 1990s. Since the 1990s there has been a third Morris the Cat, eating 9Lives and making television appearances from time to time.

Throughout his history, Morris the Cat has appeared in two movies, acted in public service announcements for animal shelters and pet adoption, and even ran for president in 1988—well, it wasn't serious, but it was fun and Morris seemed to love the attention!

Morris may not have been as popular as Lassie, but he proved that cats are just as loved by millions of people. And since three cats have played Morris, you can say so far he's had 27 lives.

Supercalifragilisticexpialidocious

Try saying that "word" real fast three times in a row. Actually, trying to say it at all is difficult. You're probably thinking that it's just a silly word that doesn't really mean anything, but you'd be wrong—well, sort of.

The word supercalifragilisticexpialidocious first became famous when Dick Van Dyke and Julie Andrews sang a song about it in the 1964 Disney musical, *Mary Poppins*. There's a good chance you've seen the recent sequel to the original *Mary Poppins*, or maybe you've seen the original and wondered what this silly word was and what it meant.

Well, it was actually around long before Van Dyke and Andrews uttered those famous words on the silver screen.

According to the *Oxford English Dictionary*, in 1931 it was defined as a word that means "all that is grand, great, glorious, splendid, superb, wonderful." The spelling slightly changed during the three-plus decades before *Mary Poppins* came out, but it generally meant the same thing.

In the 1940s and '50s, it became one of those words that kids like to use to separate themselves from their parents' generation such as cool, groovy, awesome, or based.

So how did supercalifragilisticexpialidocious make it into *Mary Poppins*? After all, the character of Mary Poppins originally came from a book and she never did song and dance routines. Well, when *Mary Poppins* was turned into a musical, brothers Robert and Richard Sherman wrote all the songs. The Sherman brothers later said that they learned the word when they were kids, although they didn't know it had any meaning at the time. It was just a funny-sounding word that stuck with them into their adulthoods.

The strangeness of the word was one of the reasons for *Mary Poppins* being such a hit. It's clearly one of the most memorable scenes in the movie and the song itself got extensive radio play. It made it to the *Billboard* Hot 100 and Adult Contemporary charts.

As difficult as supercalifragilisticexpialidocious is to say, it isn't the longest known word in the English language. The longest published word is the name for a specific chemical at nearly 2,000 letters. Much too long for me to write here!

The longest word to appear in a major dictionary is:-

- pneumonoultramicroscopicsilicovolcanokoniosis, which is the name of a disease. At 45 letters, pneumonoultramicroscopicsilicovolcanokoniosis beats supercalifragilisticexpialidocious by nine letters.

Luckily for you, the chances that you'll have to use either of these words anytime soon are slim to none.

The Vikings Invented
Skating, Skiing, and Sledding

If you live in a colder area in North America, Europe, or Asia, or a high mountainous region throughout the world, then there's a good chance you like winter sports and activities. Winters can get pretty long so it's important to get out of the house and get some fresh air, building snowmen and snow forts, having snowball fights with your friends and neighbors, or playing one of the many winter sports available.

Where I grew up, hockey was a fun sport we played on neighborhood rinks, and if we didn't have enough kids for a game, we just skated around. We also liked to ski, cross-country and downhill, and of course, sledding.

You may find it hard to believe, but the Vikings are responsible for inventing or making popular skating, skiing, *and* sledding. The Vikings are known for being fearless raiders and conquerors in Europe's Middle Ages, but they were also big fans of winter sports. Often, it was those winter activities that helped them to raid and conquer other regions.

The Vikings came from the region of Europe known as Scandinavia, which is today the countries of Norway, Sweden, Denmark, Iceland, and Finland. Scandinavia is full of lakes and forests, and since it's so far to the north, those lakes are frozen during much of the winter.

So if Lars the Viking king, together with you, wanted to raid Erik the Viking king on the other side of the mountain during the winter, beating a track through the snow could take a long time and could be very dangerous.

If Lars' army was slogging through the snow at a slow pace, Erik and his boys could pounce on them more easily, right?

So, the Vikings began inventing ways to travel more easily through the snow and ice.

The first ice skates were invented in Finland about 2,000 BCE, almost 3,000 years before the Vikings were around. Skating spread across Scandinavia so that by the time the Vikings began building kingdoms in the 700s CE it was an everyday part of Scandinavian culture.

Sledding also developed in Scandinavia, as Scandinavians used sleds to move goods and people across heavy snow and icy lakes. Some of the earliest known sleds were found with the famous Osberg Ship. This was a huge Viking ship that sailed around Europe in the early 800s CE.

The Vikings eventually combined their knowledge of skates and sleds to make some of the world's first sleighs. A Viking Era story known as "The History of Halvdan the Black" tells how the Viking King Halvdan (820-860 CE) tried traversing a frozen lake in a sleigh but met with tragic consequences:

> "Halvdan the Black drove on a sledge from the feast in Hadeland and his route so lay that he went over the lake of Rand. It was in the spring and it was thawing. They drove over Rökensvik; during the winter there had been a cattle branding and when the dung had fallen on the ice it had eaten itself in during the thaw. And when the

king drove over it, the ice burst under him, so that he was drowned and many men with him."

The Vikings are also responsible for making skiing popular. As with skating, skiing was invented in Scandinavia long before the Vikings, but the Vikings used skiing—especially what we call cross-country skiing—to move quickly across wooded areas with heavy snow.

Viking skis were pretty simple. They were pieces of wood that were cut down and cured to various lengths depending on the maker. In fact, the word "ski" is an ancient word from Norse (the language of the Vikings) that means "split wood."

So the next time you're sledding, skiing, or skating with your friends or family, you'll know that the equipment you're using became possible due to the conquering and warlike nature of the Vikings.

Two-Headed Snakes

Human history is full of many myths and legends about creatures with two or more heads. Perhaps the most famous of all these multi-headed monsters was the hydra of Greek mythology. According to the myth, if the hydra lost one of its heads, it grew another.

Thankfully, the hydra is only a myth and we don't have to deal with a multi-headed snake, but the truth is most myths are based on some reality.

Throughout the animal kingdom, which includes us humans, numerous species exhibit the condition known as *polycephaly*. I know that looks like a million-dollar word, but it's really just two words: poly, which is the Greek word meaning "many," and cephaly, which is another Greek word that means "head."

So polycephaly just means "many heads," but in most cases, it just involves two heads.

Yes, there are creatures born with two heads, even some people...sort of.

Sometimes human twins are born that haven't completely separated in their mother's womb. These are known as *conjoined twins*. Conjoined twins can be conjoined in several different areas of the body, but when twins are born with two arms, legs, *and* heads, they have polycephaly. A set of conjoined twins with polycephaly has the appearance of being one person with two heads.

Of course, this is extremely rare in humans, but not entirely unheard of. You may know about Abigail and Brittney Hensel from their show *Abby & Brittney* on The Learning Channel. If you aren't familiar with the Hensel twins, they do actually look like one person with two heads. Although polycephaly is extremely rare in humans and unfortunately usually leads to a short life, it isn't so rare in some animals.

Polycephaly is most common in snakes and turtles, but those animals rarely live long with the condition.

Some snakes with two heads have been captured, cared for, and kept alive for several years by scientists. An albino rat snake named 'We' was kept alive for eight years and black rat snake lived for 20 years. Scientists have even confirmed that some of these two-headed snakes reproduced normal offspring.

Scientists have tried to find the source of polycephaly, but have so far had no success. They hope that if they can find what causes polycephaly then they can prevent it from happening.

In the meantime, if you ever come across an animal or person with polycephaly, don't be afraid. There is nothing dangerous about the condition and it's not contagious. Besides, two heads are better than one!

Do Dogs Dream?

If you have a dog, you've probably watched him or her sleeping. And if you've watched your dog sleeping enough, you've seen some twitching and rolling about happen. I know the first time I saw my dog twitching in his sleep I thought, "Jake must be dreaming!"

But is it possible that dogs, and cats for that matter, can dream while they sleep?

Well, I asked my parents and even some teachers if dogs dreamed, but no one really seemed to have an answer. Many said that the twitching is just reflexes, while others said that yes, dogs do dream. Keep in mind though, it was a long, long time ago since I was a kid. Things have changed and we know a lot more about animal biology now.

In more recent years, scientists have concluded that all mammals, which includes dogs *and* cats, go through a sleep cycle that is very much like ours. The most important part of the sleep cycle in terms of dreaming is known as "rapid eye movement" or REM. Although your eyelids are usually closed during REM, your eyes are darting around because your brain is working just as much as when you're awake.

REM is also the sleep phase when you have the clearest dreams.

Since dogs also experience REM, studies have shown that your puppy is really having a dream when you see him or her twitching on the floor.

So what do dogs dream about?

You know that dreams can be pretty strange sometimes and often confusing, but they usually involve places, people, and things from your everyday life. Scientists believe the same goes for dogs. As one scientist said: "What we've basically found is that dog's dream of doggy things."

Scientists also believe that small dogs dream more than large dogs, but large dogs have longer dreams.

There's no way to say for sure what your dog is dreaming about, but researchers believe that since dogs do dream then they sometimes probably have bad dreams or nightmares. If you've ever seen a dog dreaming, then you've probably also watched as the dog had what appeared to be a nightmare. The poor pup starts rolling around the floor, pawing at their face. As much as you may want to protect your doggo from bad dreams, though, the experts say to let them get through it on their own.

Just be there to pet your puppy when they wake up to let them know they're safe.

So now we know that Fido dreams, what about Fluffy?

Well, since cats are mammals like dogs and humans, the same rules apply. If you've been around enough cats, you're sure to have seen them sleeping (they do sleep all the time, right?) and should've noticed them twitching, much the same as dogs do when they sleep.

And since cats are as intelligent as dogs (we'll get to that debate a little later in this book), they also are capable of having fairly detailed dreams but about very catlike things. The primary difference is that cats sleep less during any sleep period. A cat will awaken, get up, get something to eat, or use the cat box, and then go back to sleep to dream of catching mice.

We all love our pets because in many ways they're a lot like us. Now we know that dreaming is another thing we share with our beloved furry friends.

Why *Star Wars* Is Fake

Chances are you've seen the latest *Star Wars* movies and loved them. It's also likely that you watched them with your parents, who enjoyed the prequel trilogy that came out in the late 1990s and early 2000s.

Or maybe you've even watched the original trilogy with your parents and grandparents.

There's no doubt that the *Star Wars* movies have become a big part of our modern society, but so too have other space-themed science fiction series such as *Star Trek, Buck Rogers,* and *Battlestar Galactica* (the last two are a bit before your time, but if you have a chance, check them out on Prime, Netflix, or YouTube).

Science fiction is popular because it combines so many aspects of good entertainment: action, adventure, and special effects, just to name a few. We all know that the alien creatures in the movies don't exist (or at least we hope they don't!) and that we're still years away from having cool laser guns and space ships that travel faster than light speed. Yet there are some common things in those movies that are just plain impossible.

I mean scientifically impossible!

Let's take a look at the most magnificent of all scenes in any space-themed science fiction show — the spaceship battle.

It's absolutely the most awesome part of any space movie, right? You have spaceships chasing each other, shooting laser cannons, and blowing up. The special effects make it seem so cool, and so real.

Except it's not.

No, those explosions you see and hear couldn't possibly be seen and heard in space.

Let's start with those awesome-looking balls of fire that shoot out from exploding spaceships. All of that may look really cool, but the reality is that fire needs oxygen and in space, there is very little oxygen. It's possible to create flames in space but not the sort of big fire explosions you see in the movies.

So then what about the loud sounds from the explosions?

Well, sounds travel on waves, much like light or heat. Sound is produced and literally "rides the waves" until the waves grow weak and dissolve. Unlike light and heat, though, soundwaves need to attach themselves to microscopic molecules.

The molecules can be of anything and, on Earth, there are plenty of molecules to go around. In space, there are molecules, but they are few and far between. So sounds can be made in space, but they are immediately dispersed in the vacuum of space.

Does this mean that things can't blow up in space? No, it doesn't mean that at all, just that if you happened to be an astronaut doing a spacewalk outside of your ship when it exploded, you probably wouldn't hear anything and would only see some blinding lights.

In other words, it wouldn't look anywhere near as cool as the *Star Wars* movies.

The Wonderful World of Disney

The school day can be long and boring. Sure, there are some classes you like and you have plenty of fun with your friends, but after a long day, you're ready to get home, sit on your couch with your dog or cat, and watch some TV.

And there's a good chance the first channel you put it on is the Disney Channel.

Since 1983, the Disney Channel has shown classic cartoons, Disney films, and more recently, original programming for kids of all ages. Because the Disney Channel appeals to young kids and teenagers, it's one of the most popular cable channels in the United States and is on in several countries around the world.

Chances are, you've watched some of the classic Disney moves with your parents and grandparents. You've probably seen *The Little Mermaid*, *Bambi*, and *Cinderella* just as many times as you've seen the more recent shows and movies on the Disney Channel. Disney has probably been a big part of your childhood, as it was for your parents and grandparents.

So what do you really know about the wonderful world of Disney?

The Disney Channel gets its name from the founder of the Disney Corporation, Walter Disney, better known as "Walt" Disney. Disney was born in 1901 in Chicago, Illinois to a middle-class family and moved around the Midwest for most of his childhood. Walt displayed a talent for drawing and art at a young age, but what separated him from most other artists was his imagination.

Walt Disney had an incredible ability to develop storybook characters and entire worlds and put them into interesting stories that the entire family could enjoy, together. Some of Disney's characters and stories were entirely from his imagination, such as Dumbo, while others, such as Snow White and Cinderella, were taken from European folk tales and mythology.

But of course, Disney's most famous creation was Mickey Mouse.

Disney came up with the idea of Mickey Mouse in the late 1920s, and by 1928, Mickey made his first appearance in a film. By the 1930s, kids all over the world were enjoying cartoons about Mickey, Minnie, Goofy, Pluto, and all the Disney characters.

And as great of an artist and writer as Disney was, he was an equally impressive businessman.

The world of Disney may have sprung from the genius mind and heart of Walt Disney, but his business abilities made those films and cartoons world famous.

After establishing Disney Brothers Studio with his brother Roy in Los Angeles, California in the 1920s, Walt went beyond animated films and cartoons, bringing his creative genius and imagination to even more people around the world.

The next big step forward for Disney was opening the now-famous amusement park Disneyland in Anaheim, California in 1955. Disneyland proved to be an immediate financial success, but more importantly, it attracted millions of kids and their families to the theme park. The Disneyland theme park helped not only to expand Disney's vision throughout the world but also the idea of theme parks generally.

Most other theme parks and amusement parks today were built after Disneyland and were directly influenced by it.

So the next time you come home from school, open a can of soda, and watch your favorite show on the Disney Channel, remember that everything you're watching is the result of the wonderful imagination and talent of Walt Disney.

What's Wrong with Liver?

One of the toughest parts about growing up is doing things you don't want to do (I'll let you in a little secret, it's pretty much the same once you're an adult!).

You have to go to school.

You have to do your homework.

And you have to eat the food your parents put in front of you.

Unfortunately, you can't eat pizza, cheeseburgers, and ice cream all the time. (That makes me think about what mixing them all in the same bowl would taste like!)

Yes, you have to eat your peas, or even worse, broccoli. Or worst of all, liver. I know you're thinking, as I did when I was your age, "What's the deal with liver anyway?"

Well, as much as you may think your parents are gleefully torturing you by making you eat liver, they have your best interests in mind. The liver is an internal organ that all vertebrae animals have that helps detoxify the body. The liver you eat can come from a variety of different animals—pigs, cows, fish, lambs, and various birds—but the most common type found in stores are from cows and cod. Liver is a good source of iron, copper, and vitamins A and B.

In other words, liver is good for you, and you might notice that more than a few adults actually seem to like it. I know you're wondering how that can be since it's almost universally hated by kids.

The answer to that isn't quite clear but food scientists (yes, there is such a thing) think they have a few answers.

As humans, no matter our backgrounds, we all seem to have a natural attraction toward sweet and fatty foods. This is why almost everyone likes ice cream and pizza. On the other hand, bitter foods are almost universally hated.

When it comes to liver, it generally has a very strong flavor. You've probably heard the saying, "everything tastes like chicken," right? Well, that doesn't apply to liver—even chicken liver! Since the livers of different animals are routinely eaten, the taste does in fact vary. Calf liver is generally thought to be the best tasting, while full-grown cow liver has a very strong taste, too much for most kids.

Scientists also point out that our food tastes change throughout our lives. Kids tend to be a bit more finicky about what they eat, and when they reach adulthood, their palette widens. Foods you hate now – well, you might actually like in ten years.

So the next time you mom or dad puts a plate of steaming liver in front of your face, just remember that it's going to help you grow into a healthy adult. Also, remember that, as difficult as it might be to believe, you might end up liking liver one day soon!

Mummify a Hotdog!

I don't know about you, but I've always thought mummies were the coolest movie monsters. I mean, you have the ancient Egyptian pharaoh (or priest) who's been brought back to life by some mysterious spells. And once he's been awakened, only the knowledge of ancient Egypt can put him back in his tomb!

Thankfully, those are only movies and we don't have to deal with 3,000-year-old mummies terrorizing us. But you do know mummification was an actual thing, right?

The ancient Egyptians were among the first people in the world to write extensively about an afterlife. They believed that when you died, all the goods and material objects in your tomb magically appeared in the next life, which also included their bodies.

The mummification process was long and involved a combination of science and religion. The internal organs, minus the heart, were removed and placed in vessels known as canopic jars. The body was then soaked in a substance known as *natron* for several weeks before it was wrapped in linen and placed in its tomb.

Natron was the most important ingredient. It was what preserved mummies and allowed them to come back to life later…just kidding! But it did preserve them enough to be studied by scientists and for us to see them today in museums.

So you might be thinking, "What's natron? That sounds like some kind of magical ingredient."

As exotic as the name natron may sound, it's a naturally occurring mineral that can be found in deserts and mountain ranges around the world. The active ingredient in natron, which makes it preserve human tissue, is sodium bicarbonate. Most naturally occurring deposits of natron throughout are comprised of about 17% sodium bicarbonate. And sodium bicarbonate is the active ingredient in baking soda.

So, now that you know a little about the background of mummification, let's do a fun little mummification experiment. You'll need a hotdog, a fairly deep Tupperware container that's a bit longer than the hotdog, and an unopened box of baking soda.

First, measure the length and girth of the hotdog. Then weigh it. Make sure to write those measurements down because they'll be important later.

Next, open the fresh box of baking soda and pour about an inch of it across the bottom of the Tupperware container. Then put the hotdog in the container and pour about another inch of baking soda on top of the hotdog.

Finally, put the lid on the container, making sure that it is tightly sealed, and place the container in a dark, dry location for a week. The ancient Egyptians did the same with the mummies they made. After soaking the bodies in natron, they would let them dry out in dark, dry warehouses.

After a week, open the container and remove the hotdog. You should immediately notice that your hotdog has become much darker and possibly smaller. Measure the hotdog and record your observations to see just how much, if at all, the hotdog has shrunk.

If you want to keep going with the experiment, simply empty the baking soda from the Tupperware container, clean the container, and add fresh baking soda. Put the hotdog back in the container, cover it with baking soda, and put the container in a dark, dry place for another week.

In no time, you'll be an expert hotdog mummifier! But more importantly, you'll have learned a bit about how ancient people knew and used science. To the Egyptians, natron was a gift from the gods, and now that you have learned how to mummify a hotdog, you too can share in that gift.

A Talking Horse Once Ruled Television

You know that Lassie was the top dog in film and TV for some time and that Morris was the cat about town in the 1980s, but did you know that, for about five years, a horse was the most popular pet on television? From 1961 to 1966, millions of Americans—probably your grandparents included, tuned in every week to watch *Mister Ed*.

Now *Mister Ed* wasn't your ordinary show about a smarter than normal pet.

No, Mister Ed the horse, who was the main star of the show, *was* smarter than everyone on the show. In fact, Mister Ed was so smart that he could talk, although he only spoke to his lovable yet somewhat naïve owner, Wilbur.

To call Wilbur Mr. Ed's owner isn't quite accurate, though.

In the show, Wilbur bought a new home that happened to come with a horse. Wilbur wasn't particularly crazy about owning a horse, but when Mister Ed spoke to him, he decided that there was no way he could part with the palomino (a type of golden house with a cream or white mane and tail). From that point on, Wilbur and Mister Ed were inseparable, with the pair getting involved in silly high jinx every week.

One week, Mister Ed tried out for the Los Angeles Dodgers.

In other episodes, Mister Ed learned how to drive and even fly an airplane.

Then there was the episode where Mister Ed started a one-man band.

And who can forget when Mister Ed painted stripes on himself to pose as a zebra so he could live in a zoo!

Well, you get the point. *Mister Ed* was the kind of show that everyone in the family could enjoy. It was also a hit because it combined the popular farm/Western-orientated TV shows of the time with a touch of the supernatural. But there's little doubt about who made the show so popular—Mister Ed himself.

So who was the real Mister Ed and how did the directors of the show get him to look like he was really talking and interacting with the human characters?

Mister Ed was a handsome palomino whose real name was "Bamboo Harvester." He was born in sunny southern California in 1949. As a bright and handsome pony living in the middle of the entertainment industry, it was only a matter of time before Bamboo Harvester's star would shine!

Bamboo Harvester was discovered by Hollywood animal trainer Les Hilton, who noted the horse's ability to get along with humans and to follow directions on cue.

When *Mister Ed* went into production and Bamboo Harvester was hired for the lead role, it was up to Hilton to figure out how to get the horse to do various things on cue. Surprisingly, it proved to be easier than originally thought.

Bamboo Harvester followed directions quite well, as he was intelligent and always looking to please Hilton and his costars, especially Alan Young, who played Wilbur. The toughest part was getting Bamboo's mouth to move along with the words he spoke. Mister Ed's lines were said by voice actor Allan "Rocky" Lane, who later became known as the "voice of Mister Ed." Still, it was important to the show's directors to make the talking horse look as real as possible.

Remember, this was decades before CGI.

Originally, Hilton originally got Bamboo to appear to be talking by using a thin nylon thread in his mouth. When it was time for Mister Ed's lines, Hilton would pull on the nylon to go along with the words already recorded by Lane.

But apparently, Bamboo Harvester was almost as smart as his TV character. Hilton was soon able to get Bamboo to move his lips by tapping on his hoof. After a while, Bamboo began following Young's cue by moving his lips whenever he stopped talking.

After *Mister Ed* went off the air, Bamboo Harvester retired to a comfortable life in an upscale stable. He died in 1970 and was buried on a ranch in Oklahoma.

There has been talk of creating a new *Mister Ed* TV show or movie, but most agree that it wouldn't be the same without Bamboo Harvester.

The Amazing Brain

What separates humans from other animals? This question has been asked and debated for centuries, probably back to prehistoric times. Some people look at visible biology for an answer and say that our ability to stand and walk on two legs (bipedalism) sets us apart from all other animals.

Others, though, may look at the question from a more emotional angle. These people would say humans' ability to empathize and feel sorry for others separates us from animals. To add to this, they would say that only humans are known to cry.

But maybe most would take the intellectual perspective. Humans are separated from the rest of the animal kingdom because simply put, we're just smarter. Our brains are usually bigger, always more developed, and we can retain the equivalent of libraries in our minds. Only humans have mastered language, and from language, we have created science, art, and organized society.

And all of this is only possible with the high-functioning human brain.

The average human brain weighs only about three pounds, which may not sound like much, but it is the largest brain relative to body size among all vertebrae animals (mammals, fish, and birds). Although brain size does matter to a certain degree, as human brains are larger than most other animals' brains, scientists have found that the proportion is more important in terms of intelligence.

For instance, whales have larger brains than humans, but the ratio of their brain size to their overall mass is much smaller.

Other factors also influence the human brain's superiority in the animal kingdom.

Generally speaking, the more complex a brain's grooves (sulci) and ridges (gyri) are, the more thinking takes place in that brain and therefore, the smarter the creature. Humans aren't the only animals with grooves and ridges on their brains; those that have them are among the smartest in the animal kingdom.

There's nothing we can do to make create more grooves and ridges on our brains, but there are things we can do to keep our brains active, alert, and alive.

Scientists have stated that flashcards, word association games, and even some of those road trip games we talked about earlier are all good ways to keep your brain sharp and functioning in tip-top condition. Since your brain is an organ in your body, eating healthy foods and getting plenty of sleep are also good ways to maximize your brain's performance.

And of course, perhaps best of all is reading. Experts say that reading anything is good, although reading things that challenge your thinking and increase your vocabulary are best. Many experts also suggest putting down your tablets and phones once in a while and breaking out a good old-fashioned book.

As science continues to advance, we'll no doubt learn much more about the human brain. Just think, at one time the ancient Egyptians believed that thinking came from the heart. When the Egyptians mummified bodies (remember reading about that?), they took the brain out in pieces and threw it away because they thought it didn't do anything.

Well, maybe the Egyptians were right about that last part—for some people, anyway!

A True Ghost of Christmas Past

Halloween is traditionally thought to be the spookiest of holidays, but if ghosts really do exist, they aren't going to take days off, are they? No, ghosts will haunt you on any day of the year, during any holiday, including Christmas. Yes, Christmas, the holiday of love and family, often referred to as "the most wonderful time of year," is known for quite a few reports of hauntings.

There are all sorts of creepy cases from around the world of truly terrifying events taking place on Christmas Eve and Christmas Day. But, sometimes they even involve presents.

The Jones family was just your average American family: mother, father, daughter/sister, son/brother, and a dog. On Christmas Eve one year, the Jones family had a nice dinner and then retired to the living room where they watched some TV, played some games, and had some snacks.

By about 11 p.m. everyone in the Jones house, including the dog, was in deep sleep dreaming about Santa Claus.

But at about 2 a.m. Mr. Jones was awakened by something, and he soon found that it definitely wasn't Santa Claus.

At first, he thought he'd had a bad dream, but after a few seconds, he realized that something else was going on. He looked over his shoulder and saw that Mrs. Jones was still in a deep sleep. He then noticed the family's dog curled up in a ball in the corner of the bedroom, whimpering in fear. Mr. Jones got up and walked over to the dog to see what was wrong.

"You okay, girl?" Mr. Jones said.

The dog didn't seem to react, but Mr. Jones saw that she had no physical injuries so he got up to go back to bed.

Then Mr. Jones saw a shadow go down the hallway.

"That's strange," Mr. Jones thought. "It's not my wife or the dog, so I guess it's one of the kids."

So, Mr. Jones checked on each of his kids but saw that they were all in a deep sleep.

Then Mr. Jones heard a shuffling type sound coming from downstairs. It really wasn't that loud—not loud enough to wake anyone—but he decided he had to see what it was.

"Maybe some mice got in the house," he thought.

He went down the stairs and followed the noise to the living room where the Christmas tree and the presents were. It was then and there that Mr. Jones got the scare of his life.

He saw the shadow of what appeared to be a large man standing over the family's presents. But this was no man! The figure stood around seven feet tall, and the scariest part was that, instead of eyes, it seemed to have two glowing red orbs.

Terrified, Mr. Jones immediately switched on the lights, but to his amazement, and relief, the figure had vanished.

With much hesitation, Mr. Jones slowly walked over to the Christmas tree but could find no sign of the seemingly supernatural visitor.

Well, the mysterious and unwanted houseguest did leave *some* evidence. All of the children's presents were opened and some of the toys were taken out of their boxes.

The commotion caused the rest of the Jones family to come downstairs to see what had happened. After cleaning up the mess, the family was finally able to get some sleep and enjoy Christmas later that day.

Every Christmas Eve after that event, the Jones family waited for an unearthly apparition to ruin their holiday, but it never happened again. Actually, the Jones family never gave it another chance to happen, as they spent the next few Christmases at the homes of family and friends before moving away from that house!

There have been no reports of the present-vandalizing ghost since.

Alexander the Great - Really Loved His Horse

One thing that pretty much all people have in common, no matter their backgrounds, is a love of pets. We've already looked at how we've made dogs, cats, and even horses famous movie stars. Pets are truly parts of our families and have been since ancient times.

Pets began to be domesticated (tamed) more than 10,000 years ago. The earliest horses were actually first domesticated for meat before people learned that they were better for pulling wagons, and later, riding.

Wild dogs were eventually domesticated to help people hunt and to protect settlements from wild animals and other humans.

Cats…well, I guess they kind of chose to be domesticated, somewhat. Ancient cats figured out that it was a better situation living among humans where they had a constant supply of food. In return, they only had to kill mice, rats, and other vermin that threatened food supplies.

So, we have a long history with our pets. They once helped our ancestors survive and build civilization, and in return, we treat them as members of our families today, even when their hunting, working, and protection skills aren't needed.

But it wasn't that long ago that horses were still used in wars.

Horses rode bravely into battle underneath their masters, often dying right there on the battlefield alongside countless men. Unfortunately, as loyal as these battle horses were, they were often forgotten and just buried in mass graves once the battles were over.

Yet there was one brave and loyal horse that is still known by his name—Bucephalus.

Bucephalus was the war horse of Alexander the Great, the greatest general the world has ever known. In case you don't know, Alexander was the king of the Greek-speaking kingdom of Macedon in 336 BCE until he died in 323 BCE. He became the king when he was just 20 years old, which isn't much older than you. And he went on to conquer southeast Europe and the Middle East by the time he was 27!

Alexander was a true military genius and had plenty of loyal and able generals, but he couldn't have done it without his trusted horse Bucephalus.

The name Bucephalus is Greek for "bull's head." If you remember earlier, "phallus" means head while buce is "bull." Although Bucephalus was a large horse, it is believed that the name came from the brand of a bull he received on his haunch. Bucephalus was large and black, with a white star on his brow. He was a powerful beast that was believed to be untamable.

Untamable, that is, until he met Alexander the Great.

The story goes that when Alexander was only about your age, his father, King Philip II of Macedon, was offered Bucephalus for a hefty price. Philip declined, believing that although Bucephalus may have looked magnificent and been from excellent bloodlines, he would be too difficult to train.

But young Alexander knew a winner when he saw one!

Alexander convinced his father to let try to break the horse, saying that if he failed, he would pay. He was a prince so he probably did have much more money laying around than the average kid!

Alexander approached the wild Bucephalus, which could have easily killed him with his massive hooves. Instead of forcefully grabbing the reigns to show dominance over the horse, he took a different route. The boy talked to the horse in a low, calm voice. Alexander was already an expert horseman; he knew that Bucephalus was probably afraid of his own shadow.

Yes, that's right: Alexander simply moved Bucephalus so that he would face the sun and not see his shadow.

It worked, and Alexander rode Bucephalus to victory after victory. It is said that finally, though, Bucephalus' luck ran out in 326 BCE. He suffered some pretty serious injuries during a battle in India and later died. Alternatively many stories have been told of Bucephalus dying of old age though. It's hard to know what really happened so long ago.

But unlike the countless horses before Bucephalus that were buried in unmarked pits, Alexander built a grand tomb for his horse that was in the middle of a new city he had constructed called Bucephala.

That's right, Alexander the Great loved his horse so much that he built a city for him!

Some may think it's strange how much Alexander the Great loved his horse, but the fact is that Bucephalus was probably his most loyal soldier, saving the general's life on many occasions. If cities can be named after generals, why not a horse who carried the greatest general of all time?

Woodsy and Smokey

What do you get when you take people's love of animals and combine it with the urgent need to save the environment— Woodsy Owl and Smokey Bear. Although the popularity and presence of these two characters have declined a bit in recent years, they still exist. And if you ask your parents about them, I'm sure they'll tell you all about the commercials and public service announcements both stared in quite frequently during the 1970s and '80s. Your parents will also no doubt remember both their signature slogans.

For Smokey it was, "Only you can prevent forest fires."

Woodsy's line was, "Give a hoot! Don't pollute."

Many experts attribute these two characters as the force behind the modern environmentalist movement, but most people who grew up with them, such as me, remember them fondly as cute critters with a positive message.

Of the two environmentally-friendly heroes, Smokey is the oldest. The character was created in 1945 by the US Forest Service as a way to get Americans to be mindful of forest fires. Since America was in the middle of World War II, the government worried about the Japanese invading and possibly burning forests on the West Coast. The government were also concerned that out-of-control forest fires could take resources away from the war effort.

So a talking black bear wearing a ranger's hat and blue jeans was created to convince Americans to be more mindful of what they were seeing and doing in forests. Many thought the idea of a talking bear was silly, but it quickly proved to be quite popular and successful.

So successful that a black bear rescued from a New Mexico forest fire was made the "real" Smokey Bear in 1950.

Smokey Bear grew in popularity throughout the 1970s and '80s and was even put on a US postage stamp and had his own cartoon.

By the 1970s, environmentalism had become more mainstream in the United States. To get kids involved in protecting America's vast natural resources, the Secretary of Agriculture came up with the idea of Woodsy Owl in 1971.

Like Smokey, Woodsy wears a ranger's hat, but unlike Smokey, he wears green pants. The look of both characters has slightly changed over the years, as have their slogans. Woodsy's signature slogan is now, "Lend a hand, care for the land!" While Smokey's is, "Only you can prevent wildfires."

Both characters were important to adults and children alike, and by the 1970s, they often appeared together in commercials and public service announcements. The United States Department of Agriculture still conducts a yearly poster contest for kids that features both characters.

So if you have some artistic talent, make a poster with Woodsy, Smokey, or both on it. Just remember to "Lend a hand, care for the land!" and that "Only you can prevent wildfires."

Chopsticks or Forks?

"Sit up straight," "Don't chew with your mouth open," "Don't eat with your hands." We've all heard our moms and dads say this to us at some points in our lives. I know I have, and when you think about it, these instructions come down to standard manners and common sense.

Or do they?

Well, good posture at the dinner table certainly makes sense, as does not chewing with your mouth open. I'm sure you really don't want to see the food in your little brother's or sister's mouth, do you?

But what about eating with your hands?

In some countries, it's perfectly acceptable—and expected—to eat with your hands. In Ethiopia and India people often pick their food up with their hands, or they use bread in place of eating utensils. When eating with your hands, in some countries, only the right hand is used.

The fork is the most adaptable eating utensil, as you can use it in a variety of different ways. Forks of one type or another have been used for thousands of years in different cultures, but it's believed that the fork as we know it today; the table fork - was first invented by the Greeks in the 300s CE. As useful as the table fork proved to be, it took a while for its use to spread around the world. It didn't become widely used in America until the time of the American Revolution in 1776.

I guess people were content just using a knife, spoon, and their hands.

You see, spoons have been around as long as civilization and they've been used by most cultures.

So what about chopsticks?

Chances are, if you've been to an Asian restaurant and tried using chopsticks for the first time, you found the experience very frustrating. Balancing those two sticks in your right, or your left hand while you try to pick up some food can certainly be more difficult than trying to herd cats if you're not used to it. But if you're born doing it, then it's second nature.

Chopsticks have been around for at least three thousand years and are believed to have been first invented in China and quickly spread to other Asian countries. Most chopsticks were originally made from bamboo, but today they are made from wood, metal, and even plastic. If you visit an Asian country, disposable plastic chopsticks are quite common in fast-food restaurants.

Forks and knives are uncommon among traditional Asian eating utensils, but spoons usually accompany chopsticks.

The next time your parents tell you not to eat with your hands, don't argue with them, but remember that in some countries it's perfectly fine. All people around the world need food to survive, but the way we put that food into our mouths differs from country to country. Maybe someday you'll find yourself in a country where eating with your hands is not just alright, but even expected.

Them Bones, Them Bones

Our bodies are like incredibly well-oiled machines that are capable of some pretty amazing feats. Just look at some of the things your favorite athletes can do.

Every part of our body plays its part. Our brains give us consciousness and our heart gives us life. Our lungs allow us to breathe air and our stomach and intestines process the food we eat into energy.

Additionally, our skeletal system protects all of our vital organs and gives them the ability to move.

The human skeletal system is truly incredible, so much so that it inspired a spiritual song in the early 1900s that is still known and sung around the world. In fact, there's a good chance you've sung some of the words or heard them on a playground.

"Knee bone connected from the shin bone
Shin bone connected from the ankle bone
Ankle bone connected from the heel bone
Heel bone connected from the foot bone
Foot bone connected from the toe bone
Now hear the word of the Lord," with the chorus going,
"Dem bones, dem bones, dem dry bones.
Dem bones, dem bones, dem dry bones.
Dem bones, dem bones, dem dry bones."

Like the heart or the brain, bones are actually organs, and in addition to protecting the organs, they have a variety of important functions. Bones produce white and red blood cells that we need to live, and they also store other important minerals in the form of bone marrow.

Bones are connected by joints, while tendons connect muscles to bones. Cartilage is the tissue that covers bones, but the bones themselves are made from a combination of calcium, phosphorus, sodium, and collagen.

Everyone is born with roughly the same number of bones, about 300, but that gets reduced to about 206 by the time we become adults. That seems kind of strange, doesn't it?

How can we *lose* bones as we grow?

Well, most growth takes place with the longest bones in the human body, the arm and leg bones. A person will keep growing as long as the growth plates on those bones remain open, but once they close, growth stops.

How we decrease the number of bones we have is also related to growth but in a slightly different context. A baby is born with about 300 bones, but it immediately starts growing, leading to many bones fusing. The bones in the skull are among the ones that fuse the most, which is one of the reasons why a person's looks change so much from infancy to early childhood.

Now that you know how important the skeletal system is, perhaps you can also realize just how right your parents are. Yes, milk, which is rich in calcium, is really good for your bones! So is exercise and getting plenty of sun. So, put down your phone and tablet for an hour or so a day, drink some milk, and get outside and enjoy the weather.

In a few years, your bones will surely thank you for it.

The Haunted Doll!

If you're ever in Key West, Florida, make sure to have your parents take you to the Martello Art Gallery and Historical Museum. It's a neat place with plenty of cool art and information about Key West, but most people come there for one thing—Robert the doll.

Yes, you read that correctly, the big attraction at this museum is a doll.

And it's not the workmanship of the doll that bring people in; actually, Robert looks pretty creepy. No, it's the scary legend behind Robert and the supposedly strange things that people have witnessed and experienced due to Robert.

As you've probably guessed by now, many people believe that Robert is a haunted doll.

Robert is a three-and-a-half foot tall sailor doll that clutches a tiny stuffed dog, and he's currently seated in a chair in his own exhibition in the museum. Robert's face has suffered some damage over the years, which gives him a very scary look, kind of like Michael Meyers from the *Halloween* movies.

Robert also seems to have a slight grin, plus two beady, black eyes that add to the sinister effect.

As creepy as Robert looks, his mysterious background adds to his scariness.

Robert was donated to the museum in 1994, but before that time, he had at least two owners. The original owner was probably an artist who is said to have been given the doll by his German grandfather.

Now is where things get a little confusing and scary.

One legend states that a woman from the Bahamas with a deep knowledge of black magic and voodoo gave the doll to the original owner as part of a curse. Another story says that the original owner himself put a hex on the doll. Whatever the story, plenty of people who've spent time around Robert swear that the doll is haunted.

People have claimed that they've seen Robert move, change his facial expressions, and even laugh. While others have said that Robert has brought misfortune to their lives in a variety of ways.

As Robert has become such a popular attraction, there have been numerous "challengers" who attempt to mock or make fun of Robert at the museum. Some of these people have claimed that, not long after mocking the potentially possessed doll, they suffered several misfortunes including missing flights, getting fired from their jobs, getting in car accidents, divorce, and various other injuries and losses.

Most people who've seen Robert haven't reported any ill effects. But then again, most people don't mock Robert.

So if you ever do make it to Key West and you decide to go see Robert at the Martello Museum, just remember to be kind and respectful. If not, Robert may have the last say and it might not be good!

The Smartest Animal?

It's an age-old debate that continues to swirl around discussions people all ages have: "what's the smartest animal?" You've probably been involved in this debate on the playground or in the cafeteria, but believe me, people of all ages like to have this argument. I guess part of it comes down to picking your favorite animal. The reality is that scientists aren't unanimous about the list either.

Animal intelligence is measured by several things, some of which we've already discussed. The size of an animal in relation to its brain is one indicator of intelligence, but so too are the number of neurons shooting around in an animal's brain. Many animals have been subjected to intelligence tests by experts, but the results show that one particular species of animal may excel in one type of thinking, while another animal excels in something else.

So, let's take a look at the animals that most commonly appear on these lists. We'll give a little more attention to a couple of our favorites.

Generally at the top of any list of most intelligent animals are primates. Many lists place the chimpanzee as the most intelligent animal, while others list the orangutan or gorilla as the world's brightest. All three of those primates are in the ape family.

That's probably not so surprising, though, since apes can be taught to communicate with humans.

Dolphins are generally next or among the most intelligent non-primates. As you should be aware, a dolphin is a mammal, and it's capable of knowing numbered sequences, understands pointing, and recognizes its reflection in a mirror.

Also near the top of most lists are elephants. Elephants have large brains they use to build complicated social structures and to memorize things. You've probably heard the saying, "memory like an elephant." Well, that's because elephants have shown an uncanny ability to retain information and therefore can be taught things. Many elephants have even become artists!

Like humans, elephants also show compassion and sorrow when one of their herd dies.

I know what most of you reading this are really thinking, though: "Which is smarter, dogs or cats?"

Well, it turns out the answer to that question isn't quite so easy. Yes, both are considered quite smart in the animal kingdom, although they both rate below pigs. Yes, that's right, pigs are actually quite intelligent and capable of learning quite a few things before they go into the fryer!

But between dogs and cats, the matter of which is smarter kind of comes down to how you look at it.

Dogs definitely have larger brains than cats on average. And although cats were once thought to have more neurons zipping around their brains, dogs are now known to have about twice the number on average. So that all means that dogs are smarter then, right?

Well, not so fast say the experts …. and the cat people!

It turns out cats have a similar number of neurons in the cerebral cortex (where true thinking takes place) than dogs and they have a higher ratio of neurons per their size.

So with cats and dogs, the argument isn't settled and probably never will be. Dogs are better at being trained and following orders, as they've been bred that way for thousands of years, while cats are better at figuring things out on their own.

If you're looking for a cute animal that's smarter than dogs and cats, look no further than the raccoon. Raccoons have scored high on all intelligence and have about the same number of neurons as dogs on average.

From what I hear, though, raccoons don't make the best pets.

The Original Matchbox Cars

The role of children in society has changed a bit throughout history, but not as much from society to society. Today, kids are allowed to "be kids" well into their teens. The responsibilities of being an adult are gradually foisted upon kids beginning when they're sixteen, with the privilege of getting a driver's license. It's only two years later that kids become legal adults in most countries at the age of eighteen. It's even younger in some countries.

But throughout history, this hasn't always been the case. Children were expected to do their part in farming or even fighting (remember child soldiers?).

However, even in some of these societies where kids were expected to do a lot of work, they still had some time to play. You might be surprised by how recognizable some of their toys are to you. One particularly interesting example comes from Central America, which from about 1,500 BCE to 1,500 CE was inhabited by several different advanced societies, including the Olmecs, the Toltecs, the Maya, and the Aztecs. When considered all together, these societies are sometimes referred to as *Mesoamerica*.

Since the Maya left behind some writings and plenty of archaeological evidence, we know about what life was like for Mayan kids. Mayan parents loved their children, but by all accounts, it was a tough kind of love most of us aren't used to today.

At about the age of five, Mayan girls were expected to begin helping their mothers with domestic chores, while the boys helped their fathers with farming.

Boys engaged in physical training at a young age because many would go on to become warriors.

By the age of 15, most Maya children were considered adults and could begin starting a family. I know you're thinking, "whoa, that's pretty young!"

Well, life at that time and place was often uncertain. You have to remember that the Maya didn't have modern medicine and warfare was a constant part of life.

You're probably wondering if kids in Mesoamerican ever had time to just be kids?

Yes, when kids in ancient Mesoamerica weren't helping their parents, the archaeological evidence shows that they did have some time to play. Kids played a version of a ball game that adults would often play to the death. Don't worry, though, the kid's version wasn't so serious. And there is also archaeological evidence that Mesoamerican kids also played with toys.

Most of the evidence we have today of Mesoamerican children's toys comes from the Aztec people, who lived in what is today central Mexico from the 1300s until 1521.

Small dolls made of cloth, clay, and other materials were probably used by children. I say probably because the figurines don't appear to have been used in religious rituals, which would leave children's toys as a likely possibility.

Archaeologists have also uncovered a miniature Aztec bow and arrow set. Due to its size, the experts believe that it was a toy set used to prepare boys for a potential career in the military.

Perhaps the strangest toys found among the ruins of Aztec cities were animal figurines on wheels. This is strange because although the Aztecs used wheels for their calendars, they never used wheels for carts or to move objects. The wheeled animal figures are also strange because the few that have been found don't appear to have been used much.

So now you know that growing up in ancient Mesoamerica was a lot different than growing up today. Kids back then were expected to do a lot of grownup things at a young age, but they were still allowed to have fun and play with toys.

Although it's not sure if the Aztec wheeled animal figures were actually toys, I like to think of them as the world's first Matchbox cars.

Barbie Gets a Facelift

Many of you reading this probably played with Barbie dolls and might even still have your collection nearby. Maybe collecting and playing with Barbie dolls was a major part of your childhood and when you become an adult, you'll look back fondly on it. You may even have kept your Barbie collection and passed them on to your children, or maybe you may just keep your collection, just as people do with all sorts of valuables.

And believe me, your Barbie dolls will only increase in value, especially if you take care of them. So keep your siblings— especially mean brothers!—away from them because I know they're always trying to hide them, or worse!

Part of the reason why your Barbie dolls are valuable is that they've been so popular for a very long time, all around the world. Barbie dolls first hit the markets in 1959 as the Mattel toy company's early attempt to make an adult-bodied doll for children. After the roughly eleven-and-a-half inch Barbie proved to be a success, Mattel created dozens of different versions of her as well as just as many friends and members of her family.

You might not know this, but Barbie's actual name is Barbara Roberts and she has an entire family. And although Barbie is generally thought of as blonde, you could originally also buy a brunette version of the original doll.

In fact, dozens of different versions of Barbie have appeared over the years as dolls and in comics and movies.

The biggest changes that took place with Barbie wasn't so much with her, but more so the other dolls that accompanied her. Christie, a Black friend of Barbie's, was first released in 1968, selling well for many years before being discontinued and brought back again. In the 1980s, as Barbie became popular around the world, Mattel introduced several Barbie friends from Latin American countries. The 1980s was also when the first Asian Barbie doll, Miko, began hitting the shelves. By the late 1990s, Barbie had a diverse range of friends, which included a girl in a wheelchair named Becky.

Barbie has also changed with the times in terms of fashions. If your mother, or grandmother, still has some of her old Barbie dolls, ask her to dig them out someday when she has time. You'll probably get a kick out of how big Barbie's hair was in the 1980s or some of the "groovy" clothes she wore in the 1960s.

In fact, there's one thing for sure about Barbie: as the times change so does she. There's no telling what Barbie may be wearing ten years from now, or what her friends may be like, but you can be sure that she'll have a different look.

And remember, girls, take good care of your Barbie dolls because your children will probably get a good laugh out of them years from now.

Can Fido and Fluffy See Ghosts?

You're sitting there watching TV or reading a book, with your cat or dog laying at your side. Then all of a sudden your pet gets up, looks into space, and then starts chasing something down the hall. Your dog or cat maybe even growls or hisses as she does it. You think to yourself, "what was that all about?"

Some people are convinced that they know what happened. Your dog or cat saw a ghost!

If you think your dog or cat has seen a ghost, it turns out you're not alone. According to one study, up to 30% of pet owners claim their furry buddies can see ghosts. This all may seem strange, but it might not be so far-fetched if you think about it.

Dogs' and cats' sense of hearing and smell are much better than humans, so if something is there that we can't see, it doesn't necessarily mean that Fido or Fluffy can't smell or hear it. Dogs and cats also have a *different* sense of vision than humans. Our furry friends may not be able to see the colors that we can, but they have larger fields of vision and can actually see better in the dark.

Some scientists think dogs and cats may be able to see in ultraviolet, which may mean that they can see things on the ghost plane—if there is such a thing.

So is there any proof of dogs and cats being able to see ghosts?

Most scientists will tell you no. But just remember that scientists don't know everything and that science can't explain all of the mysteries of the world. Scientists also can't explain the many cases of pets acting strangely in supposedly haunted houses.

Like the case in St. Louis, Missouri, where a seemingly normal family claimed that their pet dog would roll over with glee when some invisible force seemed to rub his belly.

Or there was the cat in England who wouldn't enter the living room of the new house his owners bought. Not only would the cat not enter the living room, but he'd also even hiss and claw at the air. Finally, when one of the owners walked to the middle of the room to show the cat there was no problem, he was greeted by a deep chill and an eerie feeling.

There are many more stories like these of cats and dogs sensing some other world specter. Some seem to be nice spirits, as in the St. Louis case, but most are a bit creepy like the one in England. Chances are, if you or someone you know claims their dog or cat has seen a ghost, nothing you say will convince them otherwise.

It doesn't matter what the scientists say, some people are convinced their pets have seen ghosts.

But when you think about it, it really isn't all that strange, is it? If people can see ghosts there's no reason why our pets can't as well.

The First Vidya

Video games, or "vidya" as many in your generation call it, are a multi-billion dollar industry that has been built upon continuously as new games are released. Some of you prefer console systems such as PlayStation and Xbox, while others may find PC gaming more fun. Whatever your preference, there are plenty of cool games with state-of-the-art graphics to entice you into spending hours playing.

Needless to say, vidya has come a long way since I was a kid.

The digital computer was first invented in the 1930s, paving the way for the first video games. These early computers primarily just did as the name stated—computed numbers—but scientists quickly found some other uses. The military began using computers for war simulations, and the capabilities of computers quickly increased to the point where the first true video game was developed in 1958.

In 1958, nuclear physicist William Higginbotham created *Tennis for Two*, the world's first interactive computer game. *Tennis for Two* was never a hit; it was never marketed to the public and was quickly forgotten.

But other firsts would soon follow.

In 1962, the game *'Spacewar!'* became the first game to be played on a home computer. The gameplay was simple (you try to shoot the enemy space ship), the graphics were even simpler (two-dimensional), and the playability was difficult, to say the least, but *Spacewar!* allowed gamers to see what was possible.

And what was yet to come.

By 1972, computers and computer programming had made major leaps. Computer nerds combined their technical skills with business smarts to form companies that sold video game systems at stores. Keep in mind, though, that we're still quite a far away from the vidya you play at home today.

To say that these early '70s game consoles were limited would be an understatement. They all were hard-wired to have only one game per console, and that game was usually *Pong*. If you aren't familiar with *Pong*, it was a two-person game where the objective is to get a ball past your opponent. Each player was simply a line, and you could only move your line up and down on the screen.

Pong, which was the creation of software engineer Allan Alcorn, was basically just an updated version of *Tennis for Two*. But when I say "updated," I'm being real liberal with the definition of the word. Most versions of *Pong* were black-and-white and those that did have color only had two colors. Also, most versions of *Pong* were silent and those that did have sound only had the monotonous and annoying sound of the ball being hit back and forth.

"Blip," "blip," "blip," is what a game of *Pong* sounded like nonstop. Can you imagine that?

By the late 1970s, some video game companies began manufacturing shooting and driving game consoles, but the entire gaming industry was rapidly changing at that time. When computer programmers saw how much money could be made on vidya, they pooled their money and minds together to create companies that advanced gaming technology to the next level.

The Atari 2600 console came out in 1977, revolutionizing the world of gaming. The Atari 2600 used separate cartridges for each game, which allowed gamers more freedom and choices of games. The graphics, sound, playability, and pretty much every aspect of the Atari 2600 also proved to be far superior to all the previous consoles.

The Atari 2600 may look like cave art compared to the consoles you play on today, but it was light years ahead of *Pong*. But then again, without *Pong*, you never would have had the vidya you play today at all!

High Beams, Part I

This next story is a little scary, so if you're alone, you might want to turn on all the lights in the room or better yet, read it with a friend. Some of the details of the story have been changed to protect the innocent, and other details have become a bit clouded due to the passage of time, but make no doubt about it...this one will frighten you!

Kate worked as a waitress at a roadside diner at the edge of a small town in the American South while she went to college full-time. Standing for long hours could be tough on Kate's feet, but the tips were good. Her boss also let her study when it was slow.

Tonight was one of those slow nights.

As Kate studied for an upcoming physics exam, a news flash from the radio in the kitchen caught her attention.

"Attention, four men escaped from the state prison tonight," said the announcer. "Stay tuned for more information."

Larry the cook said, "Scary stuff, huh, Kate?"

"Yeah, it sure...." But before Kate could answer the front door of the diner opened. It startled Kate, but when saw that it was a regular customer named Rudy, she relaxed. Rudy was a guard at the prison where the convicts had just escaped.

Kate filled Rudy's cup with coffee and brought him a slice of apple pie.

"How's it going tonight, Rudy?" she asked.

"Well, I'll be honest," Rudy replied. "Not too good, Kate. I'm not sure if you heard, but we had four bad dudes escape from the prison tonight."

"Yeah, I just heard about that. It's awful," replied Kate. "Should we be worried?"

"No, those guys are probably far from here by now," Rudy said, taking a last bite of his pie and leaving his money on the table. "Just make sure that you and Larry go to your cars together and you should be fine."

After Rudy left, Kate and Larry closed the dinner for the night. They went to their cars together just as Rudy had instructed. Kate started her car and got onto the highway but almost immediately she noticed that a car was tailing her.

Every time Kate sped up to make some distance from the car, the car behind also sped up. After speeding up and slowing down for about a mile, the car came right up onto Kate's tail and flashed its high beams (bright lights).

The high beams almost blinded Kate, but even worse, it frightened her.

"Could this be the escaped convicts?" She thought as she kept driving.

The car was relentless. Every time Kate sped up it also sped up, almost rear-ending her. And twice more it flashed its high beams.

By the time Kate got to her house, she was beyond terrified, so she decided to keep driving another couple of blocks to the police station.

But the car behind her kept following and flashing its high beams.

Finally, when Kate got to the police station and parked out front, she could see in her rearview mirror that the driver of the other car had gotten out of his car and was running toward his car with his arms outstretched and something in them.

It was a gun!

"Get out of the car, Kate. Get out of the car!" said the man with the gun. Then in a split second, she recognized the voice as Rudy's.

Kate then realized what was happening, opened her door, and leaped out all in one motion. As she did, for a flash she saw the face of a deranged man holding a knife in her backseat.

Kate ran past Rudy and just then several policemen streamed out of the station and grabbed the man in the backseat.

As Rudy put his gun back in his holster, he explained.

"As I was driving home I had a funny feeling," said Rudy. "So I drove back to the diner and as I did, you and Larry were leaving, so I decided to follow you back into town. It was then that I saw the man in the backseat rising, knife in hand, so I put on my high beams. Well, apparently, it kept him from pouncing."

"And most importantly," Rudy continued. "You did the smart thing by coming here to the police station."

Kate dodged a bullet in more ways than one that night. It turned out that her unwanted passenger was not just one of the escapees from the prison, but a killer and the worst of the lot.

Kate went home that night feeling a surge of emotions, but mainly she was just relieved that she had lived to tell this story.

Ice Cream, Ice Cream

In an earlier chapter about liver and people's sense of taste, I mentioned how everyone, regardless of age or background, loves ice cream. Well, that might be a bit of an overstatement, but I haven't met anyone who doesn't like ice cream, and I can guarantee I'm a bit older than you.

The ingredients in ice cream are pretty simple—ice, water, salt, milk, cream, air, and sugar—but since the discovery of the endothermic effect is a modern idea, ice cream as we know it hasn't been around very long.

But that's not to say that people didn't have frozen desserts that led to the creation of ice cream.

We know from ancient records that the people of the Mesopotamian city of Mari used ice in their drinks more than 4,000 years ago (or about 2000 BCE). The texts state that the king of Mari would send expeditions up into the mountains to collect ice and then bring it back and store it in large, sealed rooms.

The Romans were also known for collecting ice from mountains, but they often put fruit flavorings in their ice dishes to make the world's first sorbets. A sorbet is technically an ice dessert that doesn't have dairy.

During the Middle Ages, the idea spread throughout Europe and Asia, with many different emperors and kings adding their own individual ingredients and twists to the mixes.

Since refrigeration wouldn't be invented until the 1800s, the kings and emperors were quite limited in their indulging in iced fruit desserts. They had to be located relatively close to ice and it had to be stored in rooms that were the right temperature so that the ice wouldn't freeze or melt too quickly. Needless to say, it was a very expensive venture and sorbets were only enjoyed by the rich and powerful.

True ice cream was first invented in Europe in the 1700s, although the exact year and the inventor remain unknown. More than likely, as chefs and other people with some time on their hands began experimenting with sorbet production, they began adding milk and creams and using the endothermic process to make ice cream as we know it today.

Without getting too technical, the process involves mixing the ingredients in a tub or container. Saltwater is cooled by the ice, causing it to partially melt. The partially melted mixture then absorbs heat, bringing the cream mixture below the freezing point of water.

Because ice cream was still difficult to properly store in the 1700s, it remained a treat of the elite until bakeries and dairy stores began using refrigeration in the 1800s. After that, it didn't take long for ice cream to catch on and become the most popular dessert in most countries.

It wasn't until the 1930s when soft ice cream was invented. According to one story, an ice cream maker and seller named Tom Carvel came up with the idea when his ice cream truck broke down and he sold half-melted ice cream to hungry people on a hot summer day. Another claim is that soft ice cream was invented by the Dairy Queen company in the 1930s in Illinois.

Either way, most experts agree that soft ice cream was invented in the United States, and we all can agree that it's truly delicious.

Cavemen Liked to Fish

Fishing is one of the best pastimes you can do because it's so beneficial in many ways. The exercise you get from walking around helps your body, and the skills you learn help keep your mind sharp. Not only that, it's just good to get outside and get some fresh air for an hour or two.

Fishing can also be a good way to spend some time with your friends or family, or alternatively, to spend some time alone just thinking about things. On top of all that, fish tastes pretty good and even better when you have caught it yourself.

Because fishing is so much fun, and a good source of protein, it's no wonder that people throughout history have fished extensively. Documents from ancient China to medieval Europe, art from the ancient Egyptians, and the archaeological remains of the Aztecs all show that fish has long been a major part of humans' diets and fishing has a long history as a major pastime.

So how far back in humanity does fishing go?

You may be surprised to learn that there's archaeological evidence that people ate fish as far back as 40,000 years ago. That's right, the cavemen seem to have enjoyed eating fish, but how they caught them way back then isn't known for sure. Some of the earliest fishermen very well may have caught fish with their hands. As difficult as it may sound, it's been done all over the world for even longer than records have been kept.

And there's even a word for catching catfish with your hands—noodling.

It wasn't until the Late Stone Age (after about 15,000 years ago) that people began using spears and harpoons to catch fish. Around that time, people also began fishing the old-fashioned way, with a hook and line. You may be surprised to learn, but fishing with a hook and line has changed very little since the Stone Age. The cavemen made their hooks from bone instead of metal, and their lines were made from hairs or animal intestines instead of monofilament, but other than that, it was pretty much the same.

After humans started forming permanent settlements during what is known as the Neolithic Period about 12,000 years ago, fishing became more important. People learned that fish was a good source of protein and so gathering large amounts was important to feed growing populations.

So, nets were invented and they too have changed little since.

So, when you look at the history of fishing, it really hasn't changed much since the Stone Age. People back then fished for a source of food, but I'm also sure that they fished for the same recreational reasons that we do.

Think of it this way: what better way could a caveman unwind after protecting his family and tribe from saber tooth tigers, wooly mammoths, and other cavemen?

I can't think of anything better.

I Bet You Can't Break an Egg in the Palm of Your Hand

Go ahead, try it. Better yet, challenge some of your friends or siblings to this challenge. For this experiment, you only need a regular egg—color doesn't matter—and a willing participant. I would say to do it over a sink or outside, but if the person trying to break the egg doesn't cheat, then it won't matter.

Make sure the attempted egg cracker has the egg in the palm of their hand, top to bottom. Once you're sure they're holding it properly, tell them to let it rip! I promise you, they won't be able to break the egg.

Some people have claimed to have broken eggs in the palms of their hands when they placed the egg in there horizontally, but that's kind of cheating and partially reveals the science behind this trick.

It all comes down to pressure.

I'm sure you know that eggshells are quite fragile. It really doesn't take much to crack an eggshell, does it? I mean there's a reason Humpty Dumpty was an egg; if he were a piece of wood or metal, it just wouldn't make a good story. So then how is it that something so fragile can't be crushed when it's in someone's hand, positioned top to bottom?

The shape of an egg is pretty much a natural arch. Architects make arches to support bridges and structures in buildings.

Arches distribute weight and pressure evenly, allowing for traffic and weight to pass over them. When you take that egg and put it in your palm horizontally, the same principle is at work. If you don't cheat, you still shouldn't be able to break it. But people tend to use their fingers a bit, even if they don't know they're doing it, which can throw the experiment off.

Using your fingers applies pressure in one specific place, which is how the egg can be cracked.

If you want to really impress your friends and turn this experiment into a sort of magic trick, challenge them to break the egg. After they fail, you can then show them how you can break it.

Yes, you can break an egg placed top to bottom in the palm of your hand if you do this one simple cheat. Put a small ring on your middle finger before the challenge. It should be a small ring that isn't easily noticed. When you take your turn, make sure that the ring is putting pressure on the egg. The pinpointed pressure from the ring should be enough to crack the egg.

You should be able to fool your friends, but make sure not to do it too often—or someone will notice the ring!

These Kids Ruled the World, Literally!

Many of you reading this dream of the day you'll become an adult. You look forward to owning a car, a home, having a family, and some money in the bank. All of that is great, but just remember to enjoy your childhood while you still can. With all of those nice things comes a lot of responsibility, and responsibility isn't always much fun.

There have been many kids throughout history who didn't get a chance to truly be kids. They were given the extreme responsibility of having to rule kingdoms or even large empires from the time they were very young or even—in some cases—when they were born.

One of the best-known child rulers in history was the Egyptian pharaoh Tutankhamun, better known as King Tut (1342-1327 BC). Tut's father may have been his predecessor Akhenaten, or Akhenaten may have been his brother. Either way, after Akhenaten died, Tut was the next in line to become king at the ripe age of 8 or 9.

It remains a mystery how Tut died, although he was in the prime of his life at 18 or 19.

Ancient Egypt was home to several other child rulers, the most important of which was Thutmose III (1481-1425 BCE). Thutmose III the third became king at about the age of 2, which was obviously too young to make decisions so his aunt Hatshepsut (1507-1458 BCE) ruled in his place for several years.

Thutmose III took complete control of Egypt away from his aunt when he was about 22 and went on to become one of Egypt's greatest pharaohs. He expanded Egypt's borders far into the north and south and erected several temples throughout Egypt that still stand today.

The late ancient and medieval periods of world history witnessed hundreds of child rulers from Europe, Asia, and the Middle East. Like Thutmose III, these children were often too young to make rational decisions, so they were given a "co-regent" (co-ruler) or advisors who helped them make decisions.

Fulin was a 5-year-old boy who liked to play with his friends, but when a group of Chinese princes chose him to be the next emperor of the Qing Dynasty in 1643, he had to grow up real fast. The princes picked Fulin's uncle Dorgon to serve as his co-regent, but Dorgon died when Fulin was 12, so the boy decided to rule alone.

Fulin later took the name the "Shunzhi emperor," and was known for being a peaceful and enlightened ruler. Unfortunately, Fulin died of smallpox at the age of 22.

Europe has also had its share of notable and important child rulers, but perhaps none more so than Ivan IV (1530-1584), the Tsar (emperor) of Russia. Perhaps you've heard of Ivan IV by his nickname, "Ivan the Terrible"? Well, he certainly earned that nickname, as he was known for being extremely paranoid and sometimes quite cruel. He is even believed to have murdered his own son in a fit of uncontrollable rage!

But perhaps we shouldn't judge Ivan too much. He became the Tsar at the young age of 17, and he grew up in a time and place that could be quite brutal. The Russians were constantly fighting with other Europeans and each other to the west and the Mongols to the east.

It's hard to blame any of these child rulers for mistakes they made and things they did that we consider bad today. They were put into difficult positions at young ages and never really had time to just have fun and be kids.

Not the Kind of Dog
You Want to Meet

If you're ever traveling through the more remote areas of Britain at night, be quiet and listen. Depending on the time of year, you're sure to hear crickets, frogs, and other assorted bugs and small animals, but if you listen longer, you may hear something a bit more ominous.

You may hear the howl of what sounds like a wolf or a big dog.

"Wolves and wild dogs aren't native to the British Isles," you might be thinking.

And technically you'd be right, but those howls you're hearing may just come from another world. For hundreds of years, the rural countryside of England, Scotland, Wales, and Ireland have been haunted by the sounds and sightings of what are described as large, black dogs. As scary as these sightings are, they are also elusive. No black dog has ever been caught on film or video, never mind captured alive.

But the fact is, there have been hundreds of black dog sightings over a long time span and hundreds of miles. So, all these people must be seeing something, right?

You've probably heard that a black cat signals bad luck; well, the same held true for black dogs in medieval Europe. It was believed that these black dogs were conjured up through black magic and were, therefore, more of an apparition than a physical dog.

But that's all monster movie stuff, right?

I'm definitely not saying that black dogs are demons from another dimension, but there's no denying that people have been seeing *something* across the British Isles for centuries and in some areas more than others.

County Devon in far southwestern England has been plagued by black dog sightings since the late 1600's. The sightings in Devon became so well-known that the famous novelist Arthur Conan Doyle (the guy who wrote the Sherlock Holmes stories) used them as the basis for his novel *The Hound of the Baskervilles*.

Many of these mysterious black dogs were said to appear after someone had been murdered or executed. The Black Dog of Tring began appearing near the town of Tring after a man was executed in 1751 for murder and the Black Dog of Newgate was said to haunt the Newgate prison after an inmate was murdered there in 1596.

And black dog sightings continue into the present.

In the southwestern England county of Dorset, locals claim that if you let your dog run loose late at night on a trail outside the town of Lyme Regis, it will become the victim of the Black Dog of Lyme Regis.

More recently, in 2003, a teenager in rural England reported seeing a black dog the size of a cow along a lonely country road. The creature ran off and was never seen again.

There are hundreds of sightings such as these, which makes one think that they can't all be made up. If people *are* seeing large canines (the animal family that includes dogs, wolves, and coyotes) in the rural British Isles, can there be a rational explanation that doesn't involve the supernatural?

Many experts believe that some of the reported sightings are hoaxes meant to get attention. Some of the hoaxers could be local business owners who want tourists to visit their forgotten towns, while others are just doing it for fun. But hoaxes can't explain all of these cases.

Other cases may just be people seeing large dogs that have gotten loose. As far as the dogs always being black, night time has a way of making everything look darker. Meanwhile, the larger-than-normal size of the black dogs may be due to overactive imaginations and adrenaline. In this way, the legend of the black dog has become a sort of self-fulfilling prophecy. Everyone in rural England has heard the legend, so when they see a large dog on the loose in the country at night they think they're seeing a legendary black dog.

Still others think that black dog sightings are something more.

Although wild canines haven't roamed the British Isles for hundreds of years, some people believe black dogs are either a hidden population of wild dogs that haven't been documented, or they're a domestic dog - wild dog hybrid.

Believe it or not, some really do think that black dogs are otherworldly visitors.

So, just remember, if you're ever backpacking through rural Britain and you hear what sounds like a wolf, or you see an abnormally large dog, it could be a black dog. Instead of trying to prove that these creatures exist by capturing one, though, I'd recommend letting the black dog go on its way and for you to go on yours.

After all, maybe black dogs are visitors from another world.

Polly Want a Cracker?

Do you remember the first time you heard a parrot "talk"? I do. It was pretty amazing and a bit weird. I mean, here was a bird saying words that I clearly understood. Granted, the parrot wasn't saying complete sentences or very many words, but the fact that it was saying any words at all was pretty incredible.

After all, I thought back then, "Neither my dog nor my cat can make any sounds that are even close to being human words."

Some parrots have been documented as being able to utter hundreds of words, and others have shown an ability to almost talk with humans. So how is this incredible feat possible?

Birds in the parrot family are the most common "talkers," but the family itself includes many different species, including parakeets and cockatoos. African grey parrots are believed to be the smartest of all parrots and the best talkers.

You may be surprised, or maybe not, to learn that parrots aren't the only birds capable of speech. Several species of songbirds, including magpies and mockingbirds (obviously where they get the name), can say some words. But the smartest of all the non-parrots are crows.

Yes, that's right, crows are pretty sharp birds. They're arguably some of the smartest animals of all, capable of social organization, learning, and even imitating some human words.

There are crows in zoos that are known for saying human words, and if you ever watch a murder of crows (what a flock of crows is called) for a while you may even notice them saying words.

It's a bit creepy but also cool at the same time!

How birds talk is a bit of a controversy among scientists. Well, not how it works biologically with their vocal cords, but more so *why* they talk and if what they are doing is talking as we know it.

Many scientists believe that talking birds are merely doing mimicry. Mimicry is the act of copying what another person, or thing, says or does. There are several reasons why birds would mimic human speech. Since most of the birds we hear talking either live in captivity or spend a lot of time around humans, many scientists believe they are mimicking us to "fit in." They may see us as part of their flocks, similar to how dogs see us as part of their packs.

Other theories suggest that some talking birds mimic the sounds of what they perceive as a threat to keep the threat at bay. Or maybe a bird that knows a lot of different sounds, especially male birds, is seen as the cool bird who all the lady birds like.

But those who think talking birds only mimic sounds never met Alex the grey parrot.

Alex was a cute little male parrot who was born in England in 1976 and died in the United States in 2007 at the age of 31. Alex spent most of his life living with animal psychologist Irene Peppenberg, who believed parrots were as smart as dolphins and apes.

Sorry dog and cat people, but Peppenberg placed parrots a couple of rungs above our furry friends in the intelligence department.

Alex knew over 100 words, but most amazingly, he seemed to know how to use them to interact with humans. The experiments showed that in addition to Alex being able to answer simple questions with yes or no answers, he could also count and recognize and remember objects, people, and colors.

Although not all experts were convinced that Alex was truly using words the way humans do, most agreed that he was a remarkable little bird.

So the next time you hear someone called a "bird brain," remember that when it comes to parrots and crows it's actually a compliment.

Freaky Friday, Again and Again

Many people today say that the film and television industry has run out of creativity and ideas. Hollywood just isn't original anymore. To back up this claim, they point to all of the movies and TV shows from the 1960s, '70s, '80s, and '90s that have been remade in the last ten years or so. Since you weren't around in those earlier decades, you probably can't name any of these remakes right off hand, but trust me, there are quite a few. And many of them are movies that target your age group.

The Parent Trap was one of these movies. The original version of *The Parent Trap* was a Disney movie that came out in 1961, starring teenage British actress Hayley Mills in a dual role. In the movie, Mills' first character meets her other character at a summer camp, and the two girls learn that they are twins who were separated at birth when their parents divorced. The girls then work together to successfully get their parents back together.

As silly and unbelievable as *The Parent Trap* was, it proved to be very popular with your grandparents' generation. The film was remade in 1998 with Lindsey Lohan in the dual, lead role.

The 1998 version of *The Parent Trap* made popular the idea of movie remakes and also helped launch Lohan as a movie star. One of her next major roles would be in another popular teen film that has been remade several times.

As popular as *The Parent Trap* was for kids your age, *Freaky Friday* has proven to be even more popular. The first version of *Freaky Friday* came out in 1976 starring Barbara Harris in the role of the mother and Jodie Foster as her 13-year-old daughter. If you've never seen this movie or any of its remakes, it's a bit of a sci-fi film. The movie starts on the day before Friday the 13th with the mother and daughter both wishing they could switch places for a day. When somehow their wish comes true on Friday the 13th, and hilarity ensues.

Freaky Friday proved to be so successful that it was redone in 1995 and 2018 by Disney for television and in 2003 for the big box office hit starring Lindsay Lohan. No doubt, *Freaky Friday* will be redone again at some point in the not-so-distant future.

So why has *Freaky Friday* been so popular for so long? Well, the first movie was based on a 1972 best-selling novel by Mary Rodgers, so the film producers rightfully knew that they were on to a good idea. At first, the idea seems silly, but if you think about it, it's something every one of you reading this has thought about changing places with someone. Sometimes quite a bit.

"Wouldn't it be great if I could just bypass these awkward years and become an adult?"

I thought that when I was your age, as did my sister, and pretty much every kid we knew back then. It seems to pretty much be a universal sentiment of kids in the modern age. But as fun and silly as the *Freaky Friday* movies are, they have an important lesson that you should remember.

Don't be in too much of a hurry to grow up. Your childhood only comes once and someday you'll look back on it with great fondness.

School in the Old Days

As you finish grade school and enter junior high/middle school, you probably have some pretty strong opinions about school. The food in the cafeterias is generally bad, you have some good teachers and some bad teachers, and riding on the bus can be fun and annoying at the same time. All and all, school is pretty much a mixed bag; it has its good moments and its bad moments.

But more recently, as in-class learning has been scaled back in many places, I'll bet there's a good chance you're missing it to a certain degree.

There is no doubt that school is a major part of your life and will be for years to come, but how much do you really think about it when you're not there? Have you ever thought about what school was like for kids your age back in the old days? And when I mean the "old days," I'm not talking about the '80s or '90s when your parents were in school. I can tell you from experience that those old days weren't a whole lot different from your school experience today.

No, I'm talking about school around 100 or more years ago.

Schools were a bit different back then, but at the same time, they were still schools.

Before the 1800s, schools weren't divided into grade school and high school like they are now. The type of education you received often depended on your family's social status more than your abilities and it was also important whether you were a boy or a girl.

Some of the earliest schools in history were operating more than 5,000 years ago in ancient Egypt. Known as the "House of Life", these schools were kind of like universities that specialized in religious training, but they also trained students in science, history, and grammar.

Later, in 387 BCE, the Greek philosopher Plato founded the Academy in Athens. The Academy was the center of learning in the ancient Greek world and would influence how formal education was done in ancient Rome and medieval Western Europe.

It was in Western Europe during the 1000s and 1100s that the first universities as we know them were opened. The schools were operated by the Catholic Church and the curriculum was primarily religion-based, although later it included law, science, history, and several other subjects.

Organized education was also very important in ancient and medieval India and China. In India, students studied religion in schools known as gurukulas and in China the philosophy of Confucianism contributed to a well-developed educational system. By the 600s CE in China, students enrolled in private schools to study for civil service exams. The higher a student scored on the exam, the better chance he had of landing a good job.

As much as these ancient and medieval schools may have been like the schools you attend, there were a couple of notable differences. First, there was no organized grade school as you know it. Younger kids had to be tutored privately, but most never received a formal education.

Second, girls were—for the most part—prohibited from attending schools. Some of the elite and noble girls in some of these cultures were educated, but most were kept out of school.

Luckily for all of you, though, that all changed in the 1800s. Most wealthier countries began building taxpayer-funded free/public schools in the late 1700s and early 1800s. Countries that were still colonies of European powers, such as India, also witnessed more and more schools being built.

By the late 1800s, every American state had public schools and the United States became one of the most literate countries.

In the early 1900s, laws were passed that made it mandatory for kids below a certain age to attend school.

Today, a free grade school and high school education is a right in the United States, and most countries, for children of all races, classes, and genders. And by the time your parents were your age, things were pretty much as they are today. Your parents even had computers in their classrooms, though they were nowhere near as cool as the tablets you use to do your work.

They Don't Call It French Toast in France

I think you'll agree that pancakes are great, but French toast is better. There's just something about that eggy kind of taste that really seems to hit the spot, and the name "French toast" makes you think that you're eating something exotic.

But are you?

The answer to that question is a bit complicated.

What Americans know as French toast has been around for several hundred years. It's pretty easy to make. You just take some eggs, beat them, then add them to a mix of milk, sugar, maybe a little cream, or even some honey. You then soak some bread slices in the mix, put them on a frying pan, and voila (that's a French word, by the way!), you have French toast.

French toast is a popular dish throughout the world. In many countries, they eat it as a breakfast food like in the United States, while in some parts of Scandinavia it's more of a dessert.

French toast is known by different names throughout the world. In the Spanish-speaking world, it's called torrija, while Portuguese speakers call it rabanadas. It's "Western toast" in Hong Kong and "eggy bread" in Great Britain.

Perhaps most interesting, though, French toast is known as "pain perdu" in France. In case you're wondering, pain perdu translates into English as "lost bread."

So you're probably thinking, "If the French don't call in French toast, and if *no one in the world* does, why is it called French toast in the United States?"

There doesn't seem to be a real clear answer to this all-important question, but there are a couple of good possibilities.

The first explanation is that pain perdu was gradually introduced to North America by French colonists in what is today Quebec and Louisiana. The majority of the settlers in North America were English speakers, so instead of calling the dish by its French name, they began referring to it by the name of the people who introduced it to them. This explanation makes sense, especially when you consider French toast is still called pain perdue in New Orleans. But it's kind of a boring reason.

I like the second explanation better.

The more interesting, and somewhat humorous explanation has to do with an Albany, New York innkeeper who was introduced to the dish in 1724. He began serving the dish at his inn and it soon became known by his name, John French. It may have been known by "French's toast" for a while before people just dropped the apostrophe "s."

It's up to you to decide how and why French toast got its name in America. One thing I know for sure? All this talk about pain perdue, eggy toast, or French toast really has gotten me hungry. I have to make a quick run to the store for some milk, bread, eggs, and sugar.

Llamas Really Are Camels, Sort Of

Llamas are strangely fascinating animals when you think about it…and look at them. They lumber around their pens and at times can run quite fast to get some food or attack something. Yes, although domesticated, llamas can be quite aggressive, spitting at or even biting intruders, animal or human.

Llamas are generally bred for their wool and their meat. Yes, llama meat is a tasty thing! The Moche people of South America first domesticated llamas more than 1,000 years ago, and later the Incas used llamas extensively as a pack animal to move goods throughout their empire.

There is just something about a llama's face that keeps you looking at it, and makes you want to laugh. It's cute in a sort of ugly way, much like a camel. Well, the reason why llamas resemble camels is that they're closely-related animal cousins.

Both llamas and camels are members of the animal family Camelidae. Scientists believe that the first camelids evolved in North America about 45 million years ago and then moved north and south. Those that moved north eventually crossed from Alaska into Asia when there was still a land bridge, and then they moved into Asia and Africa. Camels found today in China and Mongolia are the two-humped variety known as Bactrian camels. The more common one-humped camels in the Middle East and North Africa are known as Dromedaries.

The camelids that moved south into South America also branched off into four distinct species: llamas, alpacas, guanacos, and vicunas. Guanacos, vicunas, and alpacas are smaller than llamas, and while alpacas are a purely domestic animal, guanacos and vicunas can be found roaming free in the alpine regions of South America.

Since llamas share a family background with camels, they also have similar dispositions. As ornery as camels are, llamas can be even worse. In fact, because they can be so mean, sheepherders sometimes use llamas, not dogs, to protect their herds.

Just remember, if you ever happen to see some llamas at a farm and feel the urge to pet their long shaggy coats, or rub their weird but cute noses, think twice. Those lovable-looking llamas may also feel the urge to bite or spit on you, just as their camel cousins in Africa and Asia are known to do.

American camelids have a similar face, feet, and disposition to their camel cousins, but they lack one obvious feature—a hump. Dromedaries are of course known for their hump and Bactrian camels are known for having two of them. So if llamas are so closely related to camels, why don't they have humps?

Although biologists don't know for sure, they believe that camels have to adapt and evolve more quickly to living in the deserts of Mongolia, the Middle East, and North Africa. A camel's hump is used to retain water, which is vital for the desert region that they inhabit. Llamas and their South American cousins, on the other hand, live in regions that have more available water.

In other words, scientists believe camels developed the humps as a means of adaptation.

Don't Underestimate Paper Clips and Rubber Bands

There's no doubt that we take a lot of things for granted in our lives. The Sun will rise tomorrow, winter will come in December (or June if you're in the Southern Hemisphere), and we'll have to pay taxes until the day we die (you won't have to worry about that last one for a few more years).

We also often take technological conveniences for granted. Cars, phones, computers, and even electricity are used without much thought. There are hundreds of things you use every day that you probably take for granted. Yes, there truly are many modern conveniences we take for granted.

Great and small.

Do you ever stop to think about the science and history behind paperclips and rubber bands, or how much those two little things have affected modern life?

They both look pretty simple, but paper clips and rubber bands are relatively recent inventions. The paper clip was first invented in the late 1800s, while the idea of the rubber band has been around since the mid-1800s, but the rubber band as we know it was only patented in 1957.

That's after some of your grandparents were born!

The paper clip as we know it today is called the "Gem" paper clip. It's simply a wire made of steel, or sometimes plastic, that is bent in a process known as *torsion*. The effect of torsion gives the wire a unique shape and elasticity that allows it to do the things it does.

The interesting thing about paper clips is that although different forms of them were in use and patented during the late 1800s, by the time the Gem style became common there were no patents on it. Some claim that the Gem paper clip was first invented in the United States, while others say it was created by a Norwegian named Johan Vaaler. Although Vaaler did invent a *type* of paper clip, it wasn't the Gem clip.

It seems that the Gem clip was invented in Europe in the late 1800s and then became common by the early 1900s. A company trademarked the Gem name, but there were never any restrictions on who could make the Gem style paperclip.

The paper clip's closely related office cousin, the rubber band, also has a similar story.

Because rubber comes from special trees that are only found in tropical parts of the world, it wasn't commonly used until the 1800s. In 1845, Englishman Stephen Perry was granted a pattern for a rubber strip that would become the world's first rubber band. It didn't have much practical application, so it was quickly forgotten.

It wasn't until the early 1900s that American William H. Spencer began experimenting with rubber and the existing rubber band to come up with a new, more practical application. In 1957, Spencer was given a patent for the Open Ring design of the rubber band that we are familiar with today.

The paper clip and rubber band reached the peak of their popularity in the 1990s when they were used to organize countless documents. But as more and more companies, government organizations, and individuals have gone paperless since the 2010s, sales and production of paperclips and rubber bands have declined.

But as long as there's a place for paper, there will be a place for paper clips and rubber bands. So don't worry, there will always be plenty of paper clips around at school for you to make necklaces and bracelets. There will also be lots of rubber bands left for you to have rubber band ball making contests.

And yes, there will be enough rubber bands left for rubber band fights. Just don't get caught!

What Happened to All Those Child Actors?

You probably know that Ariana Grande got her start as an actor on Nickelodeon. After doing TV for a few years, Grande made her next big step into the music industry and now she's a household name. But Grande isn't the only big name to have gone from child actor to big-time celebrity. The music, film, and TV industries are all full of adults who got their big starts as child actors.

Before he was an A-list movie actor, Leonardo DiCaprio commenced his career in the late 1980s-early '90s American family sit-com, *Growing Pains*.

If you remember from earlier, Jodie Foster was a very popular young actor during the 1970s, starring in the films *Taxi Driver* and *Alice Doesn't Live Here Anymore* in addition to *Freaky Friday*. As an adult, Foster went on to star in such hits as *Silence of the Lambs*.

Many successful child actors faded from memory because they went on to do other things with their lives.

Ken Osmond, who was known for playing Eddie Haskell in the late 1950s-early 1960s American sit-com *Leave it to Beaver*, actually served as a policeman for the Los Angeles Police Department for 18 years. He said he found it hard to get other roles in Hollywood after playing the role of Eddie Haskell for so many years but was still happy with the way his life turned out.

Unfortunately, though, many child actors have had a difficult time adjusting to fame and money. In addition to dealing with so many temptations at such a young age, many of these kids have been taken advantage of and abused by immoral talent agents, TV and movie producers, and sometimes even their own parents!

Television actor Gary Coleman, who starred in the hit 1980s TV show *Diff'rent Strokes*, even sued his own parents for taking his money when he was a child actor. Coleman struggled throughout his adult life and died at the age of 42.

If you've never seen *Diff'rent Strokes*, it was a sitcom about the ups and downs of a racially-mixed family in 1980s New York. The father was a rich white, widowed millionaire who had a white daughter from his marriage. He adopted two black brothers at the beginning of the series, and shortly thereafter comedy—and sometimes trouble—ensued.

But there were plenty of troubles off-screen for Coleman and his two fellow child actors, Dana Plato and Todd Bridges.

Plato, who played daughter Kimberly, developed a drug addiction during the show and was unable to find work in television or film after the show ended in 1986. She tragically died of a drug overdose in a camper in Oklahoma in 1999 at the age of 34.

Bridges, who played brother Willis, also struggled with drug addiction throughout his teens and adulthood. He was arrested several times for drug and weapons possessions but finally kicked the habit in 1993. Bridges has since been an antidrug advocate and speaks out on the dangers child actors face.

If you have big dreams of making it in showbiz, don't give up on those dreams. Just remember that it takes a lot of hard work, and if you do make it, constant temptations and bad influences will be waiting for you. In some ways, those are all things most adults experience, but child actors are thrown into the mix at an early age, often with no one to watch out for them.

A Homemade Carbon Snake

In our mummification experiment earlier in the book we saw how different chemicals can preserve organic matter. Although our hotdog's appearance changed a little, it was mostly preserved, just as the ancient Egyptians preserved their mummies.

But if you have the right combination of chemicals, and a little heat, you can also radically change an object's appearance and seemingly make something out of nothing!

Our next experiment looks at how the right combination of chemicals and three chemical reactions creates a cool looking carbon "snake." Of course, it's not a real snake but just a length of carbon that grows and grows.

This is an easy and fun experiment, but since it involves lighter fluid, make sure that there's an adult present when you try it.

For this experiment, you'll need some lighter fluid, a lighter, a teaspoon of sugar, and a teaspoon of baking soda. You'll also need a pie tin filled with sand.

In a bowl, thoroughly mix your sugar and baking soda. Now go over to your sand-filled pie tin and build a small mound of sand in the middle. The mound should be about three or four inches high and cover most of the tin. Now make a divot or indentation in the middle of the mound.

Next, pour your lighter fluid on the mound. Pour enough fluid on the mound so that it's noticeably darker than the dry sand that encircles the mound.

Now pour your baking soda-sugar mixture on top of the mound, and with an adult supervising, light it.

This experiment is as much one in patience as it is in carbon combustion. Once you light it, the mixture will immediately start to bubble, burn, and turn black. Slowly, though, the black carbon will rise out of the mound and take on the appearance of a black snake. The entire process takes about 20 minutes or more.

So how does it work? Well, when you light the sugar-baking soda, it creates carbon dioxide, which pushes some of the mixture upwards. However, it doesn't have access to oxygen. You probably know that people and animals need oxygen to live, right? Well, so does fire—sort of.

Instead of burning, the mixture that doesn't get enough oxygen changes its form in a process known as "thermal decomposition." The result is that the mixture turns into a combination of solid carbon (the snake) and water vapor.

The sand evenly distributes the heat, making sure that the burn is slow and steady.

High Beams, Part II

This next story could be from anywhere in the United States, or anywhere in the world, for that matter. It's a bit of a scary urban myth that makes people's desire to help others a very dangerous thing.

There are a couple of versions of this urban myth, but both seemed to have become popular in the United States during the 1990s and spread from there to other parts of the world. Like all urban myths, they probably aren't true incidents or are based on poorly documented ones, but the fact that they seem possible makes them scary and persistent in people's minds.

According to the most popular version of this urban myth, prospective gang members drive around at night with their headlights off on purpose; as part of an elaborate and violent gang initiation ritual. You see, they're waiting for good citizens to flash their high beams to alert them that their lights are out.

Once someone "flashes" the gang member, the gang member turns around, catches up with the good citizen, and then shoots and kills them to become a full member of the gang.

This new and brutal type of gang initiation made the news from time to time throughout the 1990s and by the late 1990s, when the internet became a thing, it spread to other countries.

There were reports that "light's out" or "high beams" gang killings were being committed in Canada, England, and various countries in South America. It seemed as though an epidemic of bizarre gang violence was overtaking the United States, and possibly the world.

Only it wasn't.

To date, there's been no truly documented case of a gang initiation "high beams" murder. It's believed that there may have truly been an incident where this happened, although it's not certain that gang members were involved. As with all urban myths/legends, things got very exaggerated through a combination of fear and the media.

There is also another version of the high beams/lights out urban myth that many people think is more believable.

In this version, a serial killer drives around at night with his headlights out, waiting for a victim. The first person to flash their high beams at him becomes the victim.

The reason why many believe the second version of the high beams urban myth is that criminals have somewhat frequently used the ruse of a broken down car to commit crimes. With that said, there's no documented case of a serial killer driving around with his lights off to lure new victims.

Although the lights out/high beams killings have been proven to be an urban myth, since the 1990s, many people refuse to flash their high beams when they meet a car with its headlights off. When you get your driver's license and meet a car at night with its headlights off, remember that there's almost no chance that the person driving that car is a gang member doing an initiation or a serial killer looking for a victim.

Almost no chance.

Quitting Isn't Easy

Billy was just an ordinary college graduate with a lot to look forward to in life. He landed a good job, had a good girlfriend, and lived in a nice apartment. He really did have it all going for him, except for one thing.

Billy was a heavy smoker.

Billy smoked two or more packs of cigarettes a day and although he tried several times to quit, he just couldn't kick the habit. He told all his friends that he'd be willing to do anything to quit.

This is where Billy's nightmare began. For you reading this, though, it's truly a cautionary tale to stay healthy and remember that nothing worthwhile is easy in life. Wherever Billy is today, he's probably wishing he would've thought of that when this all began.

Billy tried and tried to quit smoking, but he repeatedly failed. He tried the patch, he tried going cold turkey, and he even tried hypnotism. None of it worked.

Then one day a friend of Billy's named Cheryl approached him.

"Having a hard time quitting, I hear?"

"Yeah," Billy replied. "Do you have any ideas?"

It was as if Cheryl was waiting for him to ask. She pulled out a business card and handed it to Billy. On it the words read "Quitters Inc." along with a phone number.

"Call the number, but don't tell anyone about it," Cheryl said and walked away.

Billy thought that last part was a bit strange, but he decided to make the call. He talked to a man on the phone who called himself Dr. Nineveh, who was straight and to the point. He guaranteed Billy that he could get him to quit smoking if he agreed to the plan.

"Okay, how much does it cost?" asked Billy.

"We'll deal with that later," responded Dr. Nineveh.

Billy went home and smoked all but the last cigarette in his pack. He decided to save that one for the morning before he began Dr. Nineveh's program. Billy then drifted off into an incredibly deep sleep.

It was almost unnaturally deep.

Billy awoke feeling especially refreshed. He put on his bathrobe and went to the living room where he left his one cigarette, but in its place were two fresh packs.

"That's strange," mused Billy. "I thought I only had one smoke left."

Not dwelling on the situation too much, Billy lit his first cigarette of the day.

Then it hit. It can only be described as the loudest, most high-pitch screeching sound you can imagine. It was so piercing that the cigarette fell from Billy's mouth and he hit the floor in pain, covering his ears.

Then it ended and a familiar voice filled Billy's apartment.

"Good morning Billy," said the voice. "This is Dr. Nineveh. Your program to quit smoking begins right now. You will not be allowed to leave this apartment until you kick your disgusting habit and learn how destructive it is."

Billy couldn't figure out where the voice was coming from, but he decided to leave. He opened the front door but was perplexed to be staring at a brick wall. Billy then lifted the blinds on every window in the apartment and only found brick walls.

Billy checked his phone but couldn't get a signal, so he turned on the TV but every channel only showed disgusting images of people who got cancer from smoking.

So he tried his computer.

Although his laptop showed that he had a signal, the only websites he could pull up were ones that showed statistics about how many people die from smoking each year and how many people get cancer from second-hand smoke.

"This is crazy," Billy thought. "Is this even my apartment?"

So Billy did what any stressed out smoker would do...He lit up a cigarette.

But as soon as Billy took a drag, he was hit with that screeching siren. It was even worse the second time.

All Billy could do was sit in the apartment, read about cancer, smoking, and eating. There was plenty of food in the refrigerator. Billy tried to smoke twice more, but the screeching siren got so bad that he actually vomited and his ears began to bleed.

"If you keep this up, you'll certainly die," said the voice of Dr. Nineveh.

Finally, after a few hours, or maybe a few days, Billy broke down and had another cigarette. The screeching siren sounded like the end of the world. The last thing Billy remembered was seeing the face of a middle-aged man. Was it Dr. Nineveh?

Billy woke up in his bed from the soundest sleep he'd ever had. He put on his robe and went to his kitchen to make a fresh pot of coffee. As he poured a cup of coffee, he remembered the awful nightmare he just had about quitting smoking.

Billy shook his head and took a drink.

Then it hit. It can only be described as the loudest, most high-pitch screeching sound you can imagine. It was so piercing that the cup of coffee fell from Billy's mouth and he hit the floor in pain, covering his ears.

Then it ended and a familiar voice filled Billy's apartment.

"Good morning Billy," said the voice. "This is Dr. Nineveh. Your program to quit caffeine begins right now. You will not be allowed to leave this apartment until you kick your disgusting habit and learn how destructive it is."

Rice and Cellphones

Some of you reading this have likely recently received your first cell phone. Nowadays, your first cell phone is like a rite of passage—it's a symbol of leaving behind your awkward preteen years and moving into the even more awkward teens. Of course, cell phones are much more than phones today. Smartphones are a way to stay safe and connected with your family but are also indispensable in your education.

After all, they're called smartphones because they're hand-sized computers with pretty much all the features of a laptop or desktop computer.

But as nice as cell phones/smartphones are, they aren't the most durable devices. Cracked screens are quite common. I'm sure you know someone whose smartphone screen looks like a cobweb!

Or maybe yours looks like that.

But a cracked screen doesn't necessarily hamper your smartphone's functionality. Sure, it may not look nice, but you can still use it. Perhaps the worst thing that can happen to your smartphone is for it to become submerged in water. Now, you might be wondering how phones get in water, right? Well, there are plenty of possible scenarios.

Your phone can be in your shirt pocket when you're standing over the toilet, and well, it comes out and falls in.

Maybe it's a hot day and you and your friends decided to have an impromptu water fight and you forget that your phone is in your pocket.

And then there are accidents. We've all spilled a glass of milk or water at the dinner table. If your phone is on the table (which your parents will probably tell you it shouldn't be!), then it can become a victim of waterlog.

What do you do if this happens? The most common remedy people will tell you is to submerge the phone in some uncooked rice.

But does this work and is there any science behind it?

Smartphones are a collection of plastic, metal, wires, and computer chips, so if it gets wet at all, this can affect how it functions. So the theory goes, if you put your wet phone in rice, the rice will basically suck out all the moisture and return it to its previous state. Uncooked oatmeal and even cat litter are said to have a similar—and sometimes better—effect on wet phones.

Most experts, though, say that the rice, or oatmeal, has little to do with fixing your phone.

You see, most of the rice remedies for fixing your phone include the added instruction of leaving the phone in the rice for a minimum of twelve hours. The experts say that the time the phone is left off and drying is what's most important.

So if you're unfortunate enough to have had your phone submerged in water, don't panic. Make sure it's off and open it up if you can. Take the battery out and put all the pieces on a window ledge where they can dry. Let it sit for a day, put it all back together, and power it back on.

This should work, so you can save the rice for your next family meal—but still, be careful when you go to the beach.

Why Is the Book *Matilda* so Popular?

Some books and book series are truly timeless. The Laura Ingalls Wilder books, the C.S. Lewis books, and of course, the *Lord of the Rings* books by J.R. Tolkien are all classics that have been enjoyed by several generations. There's a good chance you've read one or all of those series, and there's also a good chance your parents and grandparents have as well.

All of these books share a few things in common. They are all well-written and take place in either another time, or place, or both, which allows the reader to use their imagination to partake in a little escapism.

Even if a children's book is well-written and is done with a lot of imagination, it doesn't guarantee that it'll be a best seller. Sometimes children's books need to be a little "quirky."

Famed British novelist Roald Dahl wrote and published hundreds of novels, short stories, and poems during his lifetime. Dahl's talent was far-ranging, as he wrote mystery stories for adults. However, was probably best known for his children's stories. *Charlie and the Chocolate Factory* is perhaps his best-known work, but many of his fans consider his 1988 book, *Matilda*, to be his best.

If you've read *Matilda* you'll probably agree.

After *Matilda* was published, it was turned into a radio program, a musical, and a 1996 feature film with Mara Wilson as Matilda and Danny DeVito as her father. The book itself has sold more than 17 million copies and is ranked by many different magazines as one of the best children's books of all-time, so there's a good chance you've either read the book or seen the movie.

And what was Dahl's winning formula when it came to *Matilda*?

Well, Dahl wrote the book near the end of his life (he died in 1990), so he was able to draw on all his acquired literary techniques and worldly experience to create an awesome book that could appeal to kids...and adults. I know plenty of adults, especially women, who still love this book.

Most importantly, Dahl took a very average idea and added some very out-of-the-ordinary things to it. For those of you not familiar with *Matilda*, I won't give too much away, but it's important to mention a few parts of the story to understand why the book remains so popular.

The story is about a bright girl named Matilda who just doesn't fit in with her family or most of the kids at school. Matilda is very smart, and she later learns that she also has psychic abilities.

Throughout the book, Matilda is faced with many of the same problems and issue all kids face, including you. She deals with bullies, school work, and peer pressure. This makes the book relatable for most kids.

But then the book takes an interesting turn when Matilda uses her newfound psychic abilities to deal with some of those problems. I mean who wouldn't want psychic abilities, right? And using those abilities to overcome your problems would be the coolest thing in the world. It's definitely something every kid has thought about.

Heck, even adults wish they had psychic abilities!

Because Roald Dahl was able to capture these ideas that always appeal to children and young people, *Matilda* became one of the most popular and best-selling children's books of all-time. There's little doubt that generations from now, *Matilda* will still be widely read by children all over the world as a truly timeless classic.

There's a good chance that your children will also read and love *Matilda* one day.

An Owl or an Alien?

If you're ever passing through the central West Virginia town of Flatwoods, make sure to stop by the Flatwoods Monster Museum and learn about one of the strangest paranormal events in American history.

But was it really a paranormal event?

There's no doubt that on the night of September 12, 1952, a group of local children and adults witnessed something amazing outside the town of Flatwoods. The group claims to have seen a bright light land on some farmland, and when they went to investigate, they were greeted by a creature that all of the witnesses swear couldn't be from this world. It was like no other UFO sighting in recorded history, which led many to believe in the story.

Still, others believe that the Flatwoods monster wasn't really a monster at all, or even an alien, but just a scared and confused barn owl.

The incident began just after 7 p.m. when brothers Edward and Fred May and their buddy Tommy Hyer, saw a light drop from the sky into a farmer's field. The boys were just playing in the woods as kids do, sometimes seeing cool things, but they knew this was something different.

So they went and got adult Kathleen May who lived in the area. May in turn alerted a national guardsman named Eugen Lemon, and then two other children also joined the group.

After the group walked about a quarter of a mile through the field, they came upon what they all described as a pulsating ball of fire.

They also claimed that an awful smell came from the light.

What happened next can only be described as incredible. All of the witnesses claim that a creature came from the light, but their descriptions of the creature varied. May's description was the most detailed and consistent.

May described seeing a creature that was about ten feet tall and four feet wide, wearing what was possibly armor over its torso and a dark green skirt. The creature had a round head and a larger part that surrounded the head, or was some type of helmet, which she described as looking like the "ace of spades."

The creature had two glowing red eyes and two thin but long arms that had three claw-like fingers on each arm.

All members of the group claim the creature made a hissing sound and "glided" toward them.

May contacted the local sheriff and a reporter the next day, who both went to the scene of the incident. They reported smelling a strong odor of burnt metal but couldn't find any other signs of a UFO crash or the presence of an alien.

Hours after the sheriff investigated the mysterious sighting outside Flatwood, a young couple reported seeing a similar creature outside the nearby town of Frametown. Other reports followed, but none had as many witnesses as the original report.

The creature supposedly seen in rural Flatwoods soon became known as the "Flatwoods Monster," gaining national attention in the process. Whatever it was that those people saw that night, it was notable because it was one of the earliest notable UFO incidents: it occurred about five years after the infamous "Roswell Incident" and several years before the great wave of UFO sightings that began in the 1970s.

So what explanations are there for the Flatwoods Monster?

Skeptics say that the UFO was just a meteor. And as for the creature? Most argue that it was just a frightened barn owl that let out a protective shriek. Barn owls can get pretty big, and during the confusion and adrenaline rush that all the witnesses experienced, its size probably became exaggerated.

But not everyone in Flatwoods is convinced that it was a meteor and a barn owl that the group saw. There are still many locals who believe their quiet town was visited by extra-terrestrials that night.

And some people in Flatwoods believe that the aliens could return any day.

Conclusion

I hope you've enjoyed reading *Interesting Stories for Curious Kids: A Fascinating Collection of Some of the Most Interesting, Unbelievable, and Craziest Stories on Earth!* You have been introduced to a load of new knowledge, so sit back let it all sink in!

You probably have a favorite story or a favorite type of story. Maybe science is your thing, so you were fascinated with some of the 100% true science stories. Or maybe you're a bit more "hands-on" so you enjoyed doing some of the experiments. Now that you know how to do these cool experiments, you can impress your friends and family as you teach them about some little known science facts.

Since we all love animals, maybe the animal stories appealed most to you. I bet you thought it was great to learn how well-trained dogs, horses, and even cats became movie stars and how other family pets have proved to be extremely loyal.

Personally, I like the scary stories the best.

Some of those stories have been around for a while and some blur the line between urban myth and reality, but they're all sure to scare your friends at your next slumber party.

Whichever story or group of stories was your favorite, just remember to keep reading in order to always expand your mind. Studies show that the more you read at your age, the better you'll do in high school and later in college. Reading increases your vocabulary and helps your critical thinking skills, which will make you a better student. Just remember, if you do well in high school, you can get into college, and if you do well in college, you can land a better job.

Most importantly, whatever you read, whenever you read, that information cannot be taken from you. All the knowledge you gain from this and other books goes into a part of your brain that can't be taken by anyone. The information is all yours and is now yours to give to others.

So share this newfound knowledge with your friends and family and pass on the joy of reading and all its benefits to them. The stories in this book are the kind you can read with others around a campfire or with a flashlight under the covers at a slumber party. Maybe these stories will give you some ideas of your own for new stories or perhaps they'll inspire you to do some of in-depth research of you own.

The most important thing to remember, though, is to just keep reading...period! Reading is fun and it makes us all smarter, happier, and more interesting people.